Vegetarians and Custard

Reminiscences of
a Suffolk Restaurateur

Felicity Jolliff

Mary's Restaurant, Walberswick, Suffolk

First published April 2005

ISBN: 1.85215. 0831

Printed by: Hythe Offset Colchester Essex CO4 9QF

Published by: Heritage House (Publishers) Ltd

Steam Mill Road, Bradfield, Manningtree, Essex, CO11 2QT.

www.heritage-house.co.uk E-mail: sales@heritage-house.co.uk

Acknowledgements:

Dorothy Courtis, for all her help and guidance
Tracey Burrows, for deciphering my atrocious
spelling and writing
Pennie Wilkinson, for her D.T.P. input
Catherine Cook, for the cartoons and cover
Janet Fulford, for the watercolour of Mary's
Rob, for — well, everything.
Finally, I would like to dedicate this book to all Mary's
boys and girls. I trust you are all still being good!

Entrée

A few years have passed since Rob and I retired from running Mary's , a small restaurant-cum-tea room situated in Walberswick, Suffolk. Now that it is no longer a restaurant as it was for thirty years, I thought that there should be some memento of its passing. In that time it had become something of an institution, with people coming year after year to enjoy doughnuts on the lawn, or fish and chips in the dining room, not to mention our luscious chocolate nut sundaes.

In this testimonial I include a few of the recipes of some of the favourite dishes that were asked for time and time again. I was rather mean about handing them out then. "Read the book!" I said enigmatically. They've had a long wait! Quantities may be a bit vague; familiarity made it easy for me to gauge quantities by eye. The dishes will probably be frowned on by today's health-conscious public. My response to this is the same as that which I gave to a customer who complained about too much cream on her cake: "Madam, I look after your vices, not your virtues!"

Much more fun.

CHEESE AIGRETTES

1½ oz butter
¼ pint water
2½ oz sieved plain flour
Pinch Cayenne pepper
2 oz grated Cheddar cheese
Grated Parmesan cheese to sprinkle
2 eggs

METHOD

Place butter in the water in saucepan. When it has melted, bring water to boil. Remove from heat. Tip in the flour, to which pepper and salt have been added. Mix well. Return to heat and cook until the mixture forms a glossy ball. Remove from heat and cool. Beat in the eggs, using an electric whisk. Stir in the Cheddar cheese. Heat the deep fat to 180°. When oil is hot enough add teaspoons of mixture. Cook until puffed up and golden. Remove from oil and drain. Sprinkle with Parmesan cheese.

SMOKED SALMON & PRAWN PARCELS

Defrosted prawns
Marie rose sauce
Smoked salmon

METHOD

Cut salmon into 2-inch squares. Mix prawns in Marie rose sauce. Place some prawn mixture in the centre of the salmon. Make into a parcel. Garnish with slices of cucumber and lemon.

THE DIE IS CAST

WE MET HER ON THE STAIRS. "Hello, Mary," my husband Rob greeted her.

She paused. "The face is familiar — do I know you?"

"You should do. You offered us first refusal on your business when you retire."

Mary smiled. "Funny thing you should say that. The restaurant *is* on the market. Are you still interested?"

A few other 'funny things' have happened in our lives, Rob and I, usually followed by the unobtrusive little word 'if'.'

For instance — if I had not been so incensed with the Sixth Earl of Stradbroke's perceived meanness. This is the earl who emigrated to Australia before he inherited the Henham estate near Walberswick. For just one year he opened his property, Henham House, to the public.

I was entertaining guests from up north and decided that a tour around the house followed by an advertised cream tea there would be a nice thing to do. We were charged a large amount of money to be shown around two rooms by an elderly butler, who wore a black frock coat which had definitely seen better days, but he did point out to us some sepia photographs of the original hall and past members of the Rous family. One room was dominated by two enormous oil paintings of the Fifth Earl and Countess; they were so huge that they couldn't be hung but were propped up against the wall.

After much huffing and harrumphing about being taken for a ride I decided that no more of our hard-earned pennies should go into the Stradbroke (alias Rous) coffers. We would take our cream teas at Mary's Restaurant in Walberswick.

If — and here we meet the second 'if' – if Rob had not felt the need to use the facilities, he wouldn't have met Mary on the stairs.

When the suggestion that I might like to run Mary's was put to me, I looked out at the garden. On the lawn, every table was full, people were sitting on the grass, and inside people were queuing to be seated. Nothing in my experience had prepared me for coping with a busy restaurant, but I did know that there was a good deal more to it than running a successful dinner party. In the past I had smiled sweetly at friends who, after a meal, had suggested that I should do such a crazy thing.

"No" I said firmly. "No! No! I can't and won't run a restaurant. I simply don't know how."

Rob glossed over all objections. "This is a once-in-a-lifetime opportunity, Felicity. We would be fools if we didn't seize the chance."

I still thought we would be fools if we *did* seize it, but my mother's response didn't help my battle strategy.

"Well, dear, you need to do *something* and this does seem to be a thriving business."

Yes, we did have to do something. Our capital was diminishing and our future was beginning to look decidedly bleak. Could we make a success of running the business? I was very doubtful of my capabilities. My objections were over-ruled so we took the plunge.

Mary herself was quite encouraging. She would be, wouldn't she? "You can learn as you go along. The girls will run the restaurant for you."

And so, very reluctantly, I said yes.

EARLY DAYS AND SLEEPLESS NIGHTS

After many sleepless nights dreaming of soggy doughnuts and flat scones, the day of our takeover of Mary's arrived. It was March 13th — a Friday. An auspicious day to start any new venture.

We gathered all the staff together in the dining room and introduced ourselves, telling them we hoped we could rely on their co-operation and support while we learned the ropes.

"Oh, yes," they said as one. But did they mean it?

As they left the room, one of the girls asked to speak to us. She was the chief waitress who ran the dining rooms, knew all there was to know about bookings, customers, the lot. And what she wanted to speak about – was handing in her notice.

"Surely," we said "you might reconsider. We aren't *that* bad."

"No," she insisted, truthfully. "It won't be the same without Mary." This was a phrase we were soon to hear over and over again.

She stayed for the day and then off she went. We saw her a little while later working in another establishment, and pretended not to recognise her.

We got through that first weekend without any further disasters and breathed a sigh of relief. Being early spring, the restaurant was on winter opening, three days over the weekend, so we had a breathing space before the next foray. One or two of the older members of staff had retired when Mary left so we did have a need for fresh blood. A friend had started with us, but there was still a gap or two to fill, especially now number one waitress had left.

My son Colin was working in Yorkshire near Kirkby and living with his girl friend Corrina. He was in a stop-gap job before joining the Met and was not at all happy. Corrina felt in need of a change. And so it was agreed that they would join 'The Team', as we facetiously called ourselves, and they would live above the restaurant. For the moment, our staff situation was solved.

Easter hit us like a bomb. It was a baptism by fire, but we survived — frankly, we *had* to: there was no alternative. Then two months into trading nearing the summer season, the young lady who ran the kitchen came to us with the news that she had been offered the chance to run her own business in Southwold, the larger town just up the coast. It was, she said in words that had a familiar ring, a once-in-a-lifetime opportunity. She couldn't turn it down, could she?

"Of course not," we replied hollowly. At least we had a few weeks grace to find another cook.

"Another cook" was ridiculously easy to say, but not so easy to put into practice.

Another cook?

Why didn't I take over?

There was one good reason why not. I had stated emphatically when we took over the business that I would *not* cook full time. I hadn't the confidence. Anyway I was already busy making scones, cakes and puds wasn't I? So we found another cook.

The young lady left to run her café, and systematically the old staff left, one by one, to join her. But not all of them. Some stayed, for which I have always been grateful, but it was a bad time, especially when our new cook left as well, telling us that she "didn't want to work for people who were unprofessional and didn't know what they were doing." This was true enough but it didn't do our confidence any good.

Luckily we had taken on a trainee cook, Jo, who turned out over the years to be an absolute treasure. But there was still the burning question of what to do for a number one? Cautiously Corrina said: "I have a friend. She works in a pub but she is a good cook. She's not happy there and is looking for a new job."

"Ring her," I said, handing her the telephone.

And so a fortnight later Pauline joined us.

We had also taken on a youngster to train – Mel. Mel had really wanted to work with animals but decided to try catering. She went to catering college once a week and was to become one of the most efficient waitresses I have ever known.

This was the team, plus several youngsters who came in the holidays and weekends, that was to take us through the first summer. What a mountain of things we had to learn! My dear friend Benny helped out in the early days. In our first week she had gone to a table to ask the customers if they would like coffee, to which they replied: "Yes, but we would like our meal first"!

Lesson number one, then, was to assign particular tables to one specific waitress. That way she knows exactly what is going on at her tables, in theory anyway. This also prevents wrong meals going to the wrong tables, and disasters like that (yes, that did happen!). Lots of little things that are so obvious in retrospect and to anyone who had been trained.

Custard! Simple enough, you may think. In the early days when the request was made I would snarl and say: "Tell them cream or ice-cream like they've always had." Finally my resistance was worn down and I gave way. Now, hot puddings require hot custard and we didn't have the time to make it freshly for each order. In the early days it was heated up when we needed it in a jug — dare I say it — in a microwave. Sometimes this seemed to take an age while one of the girls would faff about, or it would be left and boil over, in the microwave. Oh, joy. What a mess! Finally I bought an electric bain-marie, but even this wasn't altogether foolproof. Someone would turn the dial too high and the whole lot would erupt on the work surface or on the floor, just what one needs during a busy session. Not everyone can make custard, so the cooks would make it to prevent a delightfully burnt saucepan.

Then there were the vegetarians. Every day we would make a vegetarian option, chopping, grating, sieving — the lot. Time after time it would be left, going for staff lunches or sometimes in the bin. Then I would get fed up and put cheese, potato and leek pie on the menu which could be put together at a moment's notice. That would be the day that six vegetarians would come to lunch and remarks would be made about an unimaginative dish— someone even sent me a vegetarian cook book!

Wearily we struggled through that first summer until November when we were to close completely for two weeks' holiday. To celebrate the accomplishment of trading without killing anyone or coming to blows, and for actually making a profit, we gave a staff party on the premises ending with a firework display.

BACKGROUND

What qualifications did my husband Rob and I have for running a restaurant? To put it in the vernacular: "Not roight a lot."

I had trained as a cook more by default than from any sense of vocation. On leaving school I had to do something, so I answered an advert for pupil cooks at an obscure London hospital that offered formal training. At the same time I applied for a job as a nursery nurse at St Nicholas's Children's Home in Lowestoft. I had an interview for both.

Another 'if'. If St Nicholas's had written to me first with an acceptance how different my life would have been. The hospital offered me a job there and then, which I accepted. The following week St Nicholas's offered me a post, so it was purely by chance that I entered the catering profession.

Supervision of the pupil cooks was extremely slap-happy as we were nobody's baby. Not being nurses, Matron took no interest in us, and not being cleaners, we didn't come under the housekeeper's jurisdiction. The catering manager was old and frail and found looking after ten lively teenagers too much, so gave up. Consequently we came and went as we pleased. The only time we were reprimanded was when we skived off college, then we found we were in deep trouble with the head cook, a Miss Smith, who, as I found out, came from an old fishing family in Lowestoft, a few miles up the Suffolk coast from the tiny village of Walberswick.

We were all in fear and trembling of Smithy. We were convinced she drank as her temper was so uncertain. Despite this menace my friend Althea and I had a high old time, sometimes partying all night, arriving back at the hospital just in time to do breakfast. Of course our college work suffered and we failed all our exams. I ended up being very unwell with appendicitis and somehow staggered home to mother.

On recovering I went to live with my aunt and uncle in Buckinghamshire under a much stricter regime. Here I rose to the dizzy heights of head cook at Southern Electric's head office. In the evenings I went to the local polytechnic and retook my catering exams, which I passed. All very respectable, but the shackles chafed somewhat and I looked around for another experience, even toying with the idea of joining the R.A.F. I found an agency who employed cooks abroad and they found me a job in Milan. Before taking up the post I thought I would spend a few weeks at home, ostensibly to help my mother with my bed-ridden grandmother. To make ends meet mother took in forestry students as lodgers, and yes, husband-to-be Rob Jelliff was one of them. We fell in love and I never did get to Milan. We were married from a house fifty yards from where we live now and moved to the other end of the village where we lived for twelve years, bringing up two children. When the youngsters were both at school I looked around for something to do and hit on the idea of outside catering, in those days a very new idea. I also attended several cookery courses: one at the very formal Cordon Bleu School at Winkfield, a village a few miles from Windsor, another at the Pru Leith School in London, and one memorable week with Robert Carrier at Hintlesham Hall near Ipswich.

In London, even though Pru Leith was on the premises, we saw neither hide nor hair of her, but at Hintlesham we saw Robert Carrier every day. It was great fun, especially when he hosted a dinner for his students on our last evening. A lovely man.

But this wasn't much of a background for running a restaurant.

Rob was even less qualified, having been a deep sea fisherman, a forestry student, buyer and finally a senior executive within the engineering industry, although the latter did give some experience with the administrative side of the catering business. When we were discussing taking over Mary's he made his famous remark: "After all, it can only be a question of managing and organising people."

I wish! Since then many times we have laughed hollowly at this foolish statement. We were to correct our mistakes by learning at the best school of all — trial and error.

Mel tumbles over the dog

THE RESTAURANT

Mary's, as it was called when we took it over — it later went up market as De Cressey's and as I write is to be changed back to a residential property — is on the Suffolk coast in the delightful village of Walberswick, separated from its better known neighbour, the town of Southwold, by the Blyth. If you ever find yourself there, have a look at the enormous church which has lost its roof and has another tiny church standing in its nave. Every August the British Crabbing Championship is held in the village.

At one time Mary's had been the manor, but over the years the house and garden had been split in half. Early on we had had the fanciful idea of changing the name back to Manor House Restaurant, but decided that perhaps it was rather pretentious for our homely little establishment. Besides, the name Mary's was very well known.

We had forty-five covers, in two dining rooms. As one entered the place there was a small bar on the right, unromantically called the Snug. Here people could have a drink before a meal or a coffee afterwards. The walls of the dining rooms were painted blue and festooned with fishing nets, with seascapes and photographs of local fishermen and old salts hung in what I hoped was an artistic manner. Various shelves and windowsills were adorned with sea shells, ships in bottles, and seabirds, and my uncle made us a beautiful model of the *Cutty Sark* which had pride of place at the entrance of the big dining room. Yes, I think one could safely say that the theme was nautical even if the name wasn't.

The tables were of stained and sealed dark wood, easy to wipe down when clearing. In the big dining room there were padded benches around the walls while in the Snug we had similar benches and rather uncomfortable stools around small tables. Even so on some occasions some customers were known to sit on them for too long after we had had a busy session and it was long past our bedtime. Having no cat to entice in or clock to wind, as a gentle hint, we just had to smile sweetly and say that *of course* they weren't keeping us up, although we were tempted to give them the key and suggest they lock up!

In one corner of the Snug we had a small area containing a little shop where we sold local crafts. Nothing very grand: woven baskets, patchwork, pressed flowers and such like, but it added an extra interest. We also hung pictures by two local artists, Norman Harper and Graham Peck. They sold remarkably well, seeing that people had come for a meal, not with the idea of buying a picture.

In the early days people had to climb the steep stairs to the loos but later we extended out to enlarge the kitchen and to provide downstairs facilities.

Upstairs there were three rooms which had quite a chequered history. To begin with they provided an office, a staff-room and a bedsit for Colin and Corrina. Later we turned upstairs into a flat, and the office and staff room were moved into the middle of a row of outbuildings by the side of the car park. We always referred to them as the sheds, but they were rather more substantial than that.

Our home then was, and still is, a cottage in Wenhaston, six miles inland on what we laughingly call the 'wrong' side of the A12, so we commuted to work each day. Wenhaston to Walberswick is exactly the same distance that Rob had to travel to work from Stockport to Wilmslow during our eight-year sojourn there. But what a different journey! On a good day it took him thirty minutes, but on a bad day over an hour. If it took us fifteen minutes we complained of the traffic. We never tired of the scenery, especially the view of the Blyth estuary coming down Spring Hill Lane. On a busy weekend when the flat wasn't let to summer visitors, it came into its own, as we would stay over to make an early morning start.

We also served meals in the garden, but this could be a nightmare. In the dining rooms there were a finite number of seats, but the garden – it was totally unpredictable. It could range from ten to a hundred, all wanting service. Of course on hot days it probably would be busy but sometimes we found that visitors would bring sandwiches and stay on the beach, and our attractive garden would be deserted. Contrarily, on an overcast day people would flood in. Sometimes we were quite pleased when it rained.

The kitchen and prep area that we inherited was so small I was amazed at the quantity and quality of the meals that were prepared and sent out. The main prep area had a large wooden table that one worked around. If people were organised this was alright, but if not — chaos! We removed the table and put stainless steel benches around the walls and tried to have cups, saucers, cutlery and so on, in some sort of sequence. Later when the kitchen was enlarged, life was slightly easier. Even so, on busy days there wasn't an inch of surface to be seen.

Beyond the main working area was the cake kitchen. Here I would stand making endless scones, doughnuts and various cakes and puds. Unfortunately the window looking out to the garden was also situated here, so if people wanted attending to I could hardly pretend I couldn't see them.

USEFUL ADVICE

Two years before taking on the business we had flirted with the idea of running a country house hotel. Unmitigated madness! Why we couldn't be content with a simple B&B I do not know. However, that was the year Hotel Olympia was running a seminar on *How to Run a Country House Hotel*. Off to London we went saying to each other: "Well, it must be destined." How young we were! How naïve!

I remember that Gerald Milsom from Le Talbooth Restaurant (at Stratford St Mary, north of Colchester) was there and he gave three pieces of advice. Earlier when we were *in extremis* needing a chef, we had rung him for guidance. His reply was simple: "Bugger your luck!" Not very helpful. At Olympia his words were of much more use:

- *Never employ family or friends*
- *Never borrow money*
- *Remember: one is in the business of entertainment not selling meals.*

All very true.

So what happened to the Milsom advice? Over the years we have employed both our children for a while. They more or less did what we wanted and in both cases it was only a stop–gap. We did ask both of them if they would like to take over the business, but both said: "Not likely, too much like hard work."

I have also employed friends, which can be tricky if things aren't done your way. One either turns a blind eye, which isn't good, or gently reproves which can cause resentment.

The second rule speaks for itself. When interest rates are low, fine, but things can change and difficulties can arise. The friendly bank manager suddenly becomes avaricious.

As to the entertainment analogy, before a busy evening or lunch, one can feel the tension rising and effects of the adrenaline start to flow, just like being backstage before a performance. Then the first orders go up and away we go. And yes, 'out front' some of the customers enjoy a little banter, but others prefer to be left alone.

WHAT A GEM!

Our little border collie Gem joined our family three years into trading. Before she came we had owned two Springer spaniels, Tom and Tessa, who were strictly forbidden to go anywhere near the dining rooms; anyone who has owned one of these irrepressible characters will know why.

Occasionally a few customers lingering over their coffee would ask if they might see the dogs, so making absolutely sure that the kitchen door was shut, we would let them out. Down the stairs they would hurtle, Tom barking like a banshee in his excitement. They then rushed around the tables hoovering up any titbits that might have fallen on the floor and barely bothering to say hello to the guests who had asked to see them. Sadly they died within a few months of each other and that summer I was bereft of a furry friend. Through a human friend we heard of Gem who had been rescued from continual harassment by a Rottweiler while being tied up twenty-four hours a day. The rescuers had their own dog and so were looking for a home for Gem. We became samaritans and brought her home without a second thought. As might be expected, she took a while to settle and would suddenly run off. We tried to keep the door of the restaurant shut, but it was an impossible job, and every so often she would slip off.

One such occasion was shortly after she had come to live with us. I was asked to cater for a funeral wake and I and three of my girls, drove the few miles to Holton to dispense food and drink to the bereaved, leaving Gem with Rob in Walberswick. The weather gradually deteriorated and snow began to fall. I was becoming slightly concerned, as the single road to Walberswick is notorious for snowdrifts. The mourners left and we hurriedly cleared up, quickly going on our way. This was the occasion when I looked in my car mirror and said to Patricia, "I can't see Mel following – do you think she is all right?" Patricia said, "I think you'll find she's there."

"But her car is blue and those behind us are white."

"That's because they're covered in snow, Felicity," was Patricia's acid reply.

We got to Walberswick without mishap and set about unloading the cars. This done we were due to depart from Mary's, only to find that Gem had gone missing. We hunted high and low, but the snow was getting thicker and we had to get Patricia home as Mel had left before we discovered Gem wasn't with us. Finally we gave up, leaving messages with various people to look out for our little dog and we drove out of the village with the road closing in behind us. Later that evening, having struggled back to snowed-up Wenhaston, we received a phone call from a family: had we lost our dog? Our little collie had followed them tobogganing so they had taken her in. Our relief was great. We couldn't collect her for two days as the road was impassable. The family knew nothing about dogs and fed Gem on sausages. Our little collie had a sensitive tummy and was sick for days, but she was home.

This is how we met Oliver and Daisy – Oliver came to work for us for several years and Daisy would walk Gem at every opportunity until music lessons, homework and dancing classes took up all her time. One day Daisy and her mother were shopping in Southwold when they passed a lady with a dog on a lead. Daisy looked at the animal.

"That dog is just like Gem," she said. On hearing her name Gem turned round and looked at her.

"It *is* Gem!"

Daisy went up to the woman and took the lead: she was convinced she had stopped the stranger dog-napping Gem, but the woman insisted she was bringing the pet back. Who can say? But I still have suspicions.

One summer's day we received a call from the caravan site in Southwold. Did we own a small border collie? Luckily one of our girls, Pat, was on duty and as she came to work on a bike we dispatched her off to Southwold to collect the recalcitrant runaway. Naturally Pat took the rowing-boat ferry there and back, and when she came to pay the ferryman he refused to take the money saying that Pat had been on a mission of mercy.

There was the day when we suddenly realised that Gem was missing — again — and after the usual enquiries and searching her favourite haunts we sent for Oliver. Off he went on his bike to scour the village, but she was nowhere to be found. By this time I was getting concerned, when the telephone rang. It was the lady who helped me in the Wenhaston house.

"Where shall I put the dog when I put the burglar alarm on?"

In all the rush to get off to work we had left the dog behind!

Mrs W was a lady of very precise manners and in the early days I was secretly rather in awe of her. One day when she arrived for lunch, she placed her handbag on the floor while I helped her off with her coat. Gem appeared, and to my consternation went straight to the handbag and put her nose in it. Hurriedly I remonstrated with Gem; Mrs W gently placed her hand on my arm. "It's all right, my dear," she said. "Gem is just looking for the chocolate drops I always bring her."

She was not the only person to indulge my dog. People would often say: "Do you know that Gem likes: Carrots, or chips or cauliflower." This was in spite of a note in the menu to regard Gem's waistline and not to give her titbits.

Mr and Mrs W.H. came to celebrate their wedding anniversary. While waiting for pre-dinner drinks Mrs W.H. handed me a gift-wrapped box. I started to say the usual "You shouldn't have" when she broke in. "Oh, these aren't for you. They're for Gem. I didn't think we could celebrate our wedding anniversary without giving her a treat."

Gem's favourite spot was to sit by the sliding door into the kitchen, front paws on the threshold looking wistfully in. This of course caused problems getting into the dining room, trying not to step on her, as naturally she wouldn't move. Mel, coming out of the kitchen with a meal, went to step over the dog who on this occasion *did* get up, causing Mel to twist around trying to save the plate, and in doing so hurt her back. Did the customers commiserate with her? Not a bit of it! It was : "Poor Gem, did she kick you?"

The only time Gem misbehaved herself in the dining room was when a local MP came to lunch and she was sick at his feet!

People get the impression that I am sentimental about my canine friends. They are, of course, correct in this assumption, but I am not as silly as some.

"Flick, I have an order for fish and chips for two, and could you do a fillet of plaice and a few chips for their dog?"

Acidly I asked if the dog wanted a lemon and parsley garnish.

Evidently Doglet got terribly upset if the owners went out for a meal and didn't give it the same. Master was busy designing a little cart for Doglet for when it got too old to walk – too fat, more like!

Sadly, Gem is no longer with us; she died one year into our retirement. Our successors had told us that after we left, more people asked after Gem than after us. So I placed a little obituary with a photograph in the local paper. I received many cards, letters and phone calls, proof of how fond our customers had grown of her.

OFFICIALDOM STRIKES

We had to learn to comply with many rules and regulations from all sorts of bodies — rightly so — but we did feel that some rather went over the top. In later years we learned to ask various officials whether the measures they were asking for were directives, saving us a lot of money if they were not.

After one rather unfortunate incident, I always interviewed visiting officials. The incident in question happened during one lunchtime – somehow I had managed to wangle the time off to have lunch with a friend. On my return I felt that there was a very strained atmosphere in the kitchen. What was wrong? Evidently a busy lunch had got off to a good start, when who should arrive but the fire officer. Why do officials always turn up in the middle of lunch? Are they hoping for a free meal? Apparently this one was so over-zealous he would have taken such an offer as an attempt at bribery and corruption!

It was a bad mixture: an officious official and a stressed husband, but all seemed to be going well until the visit was drawing to a close.

"Now, Mr Jelliff. I don't see the fire escape from the small dining room."

Rob pointed to the Regency-styled sash window.

Reasonable? Now you and I and the world at large may think so. A large window nearly at floor level on the ground floor. Anyone who could *walk*, let alone get down a conventional fire escape, could get out of the window.

But our over-zealous official said it was *not reasonable!* And worse was to come.

"Where is the emergency lighting?"

"We keep a box of candles under the stairs," said my beloved.

"*Candles* under the *stairs*? When I ask you a serious question Mr Jelliff, I do *not* expect to receive a facetious reply."

Oh dear! Hence the strained atmosphere when I returned. However, we did get our fire certificate, much to our surprise.

So now I had to show the environmental health officers (EHOs) around, bless them. In the beginning they were extremely helpful, showing us what we should and shouldn't do. Then directives started pouring out of Brussels and their attitude changed to one of hostility and aggression. Quite unnecessary — after all, we weren't in the business of giving people food poisoning. On one such visit I had a long discussion, over the top of a rubbish bin as it happens, as to whether the cleanliness movement was getting out of hand. For instance — were we killing all the good bacteria along with the bad? He agreed we might be, but there was no turning back. Brussels had spoken.

On a different visit the EHO looked past me at a wooden spoon sitting innocently on the side. Turning, he gave me a steely look.

"Is that a *wooden spoon?*"

"Well yes it is," I admitted.

"Don't you know that they are *forbidden?*"

"Well," I said gamely, "I haven't killed anyone yet."

"How do you *know*, Mrs Jelliff? How do you *know?*"

I have a shrewd idea that I would have done! Then an even worse sin was to be revealed

"What is *that?*" He pointed over my shoulder. Fearing that at least twenty cockroaches must be climbing up the wall, I turned and espied a nailbrush on the side of the hand wash basin, and it had a *wooden handle!*

One occasion that really annoyed me was when an assistant EHO came to help, a lass who looked to be all of sixteen years. She walked around the kitchen with a supercilious air, running her finger along the shelves and edges. I wouldn't swear to it, but I'm sure she was wearing white gloves.

Then came the rule for different coloured boards for preparing different types of food. Very good – especially after one of the girls had sliced bread on a board that had been used for chopping onions. Nearly as good or bad, depending on your point of view, as when Pat spread garlic butter on a teacake.

There could be problems – for example, if one was preparing angels on horseback, how many boards should one use? The blue board is for preparing the oysters and the yellow one for stretching the bacon, then the decision has to be made, either to put the oyster on the bacon on the yellow board or vice versa and then, horror of horrors, pierce the whole with a *wooden* cocktail stick. Now it is said that wood is good because it contains enzymes that help kill all the nasties.

There are many more regulations now than when we started. One I had to contend with just before retirement was writing a *Dangers in the Kitchen* manual and guaranteeing that it was read. For example:

Make sure one carries knives pointing downwards when one is walking.

Never leave sharp knives or glasses in the washing-up water.

Place a tea towel under a chopping board before use to stop it sliding.

Don't fall in the chest freezer or you will freeze!

Then there was the first aid: there should be a first-aider on the premises at all times. And so on and so forth.

In later years the EHOs once more became helpful and kindly towards us poor restaurateurs. No longer did we feel that we were about to be clapped in irons. As we sold raw and cooked meat they visited us twice a year, more often if there were any complaints, malicious or otherwise. We had only one malicious report, I'm glad to say. Gem, my little collie, was allowed to be in the dining rooms. EHO didn't really like it but as there was no rule against it, he was reasonably happy as long as she didn't go in the kitchen. One lady took a violent exception to Gem and complained loudly about her so we removed the dog from the vicinity. Shortly afterwards we had a visit from the EHO saying that a customer had said that she had seen the dog defecating in the kitchen. He was quite apologetic about his visit, saying that he knew it was spurious but he had to follow it up. Then he took off his badge and had a ham sandwich.

One isn't always aware when food inspectors are on the premises. Passing the Snug door Rob was beckoned in by an unassuming man in a suit.

"Are you the proprietor?" he asked

"Yes." Proudly as it was Rob, warily if it had been me!

"Are the teacakes made on the premises?"

We never pretend that we made things that had been bought in — luckily!

"No," Rob replied. "They're made at a local bakery."

"Then I should change your source."

At which he produced a biro which he had found in the teacake and his card pronouncing him to be the Chief Environmental Health Officer for the county.

And yes, we did change our baker!

OUR RULES — BUT NO 'DIRECTIVES'

We had our own rules and when we broke them, they usually backfired on us. Such as hot meals in the garden on extremely busy days. We might stretch a point for regulars, then other people would ask for a hot meal and on being told no, would get irate and say: "Well, those people on the lawn are eating a cooked meal."

Or at five o'clock fifteen people would drive in and walk through the unlocked door which had two signs on it saying CLOSED.

"I know you're shut, but we've driven *all* the way from Timbuktu to have one of your famous cream teas. Couldn't you possibly give us a cup of tea?"

One felt like saying: "Well, if you've driven *all that way*, it's a pity you couldn't first have checked our opening hours."

However, we usually relented and gave them a cup of tea. Then it would be: "Thank you, but I prefer Lapsang Souchong and my friend only drinks herb tea."

(I always threaten to put a *bouquet garni* sachet in a teapot for the latter.) The requests would go on: "I'm *sure* you must have some of your *lovely* cream cakes left." The only time we were pleased with this request was when I had over-catered with the doughnuts. They couldn't be used up the next day so we would smile sweetly and say: "Only doughnuts."

We had some terribly charming customers who always turned up five minutes before closing time wanting high tea. This meant we would be hanging around for another hour and this always happened on the rare occasions when we wanted to go out. Once we were extremely bad; we were due to go to the theatre one evening when at three minutes to closing time in they drove to the car park. While they were climbing out of their car we quickly turned the signs to CLOSED, locked all the doors, and hid. Fruitlessly they rattled the door and called out before driving off. I've felt guilty ever since.

People ringing to book a table and finding us full might ask to be squeezed in and, when told this was not possible, ask to speak to Rob as he would be *sure* to find them a table. Occasionally we would relent, but this was usually a mistake as service would suffer with more tables or double bookings than the level of staff could handle. Not a happy situation as everyone's tolerance levels were breached.

On the other hand when things were quiet, nearly all requests could be catered for. I have served cream teas in the Snug at seven o'clock just before the start of dinner, not to mention the time we cooked toasted sandwiches at eleven o'clock at night for a trio of young ladies down from London who hadn't realised that in the country it is very hard to be fed after nine o'clock.

We were told a lovely story about Kerry Packer when he was in his heyday. He had booked a table at a fashionable restaurant in a country town for nine o'clock. Unfortunately he and his party were held up for various reasons and didn't arrive at their destination until half past ten. Full of apologies Mr Packer found the owner and explained the circumstances.

"Sorry," said the owner. "The kitchen is closed, there is nothing we can do for you."

"We understand that nothing can be cooked, but surely as you still have diners here you could find us something? Cheese and biscuits would do," pleaded (perhaps not *pleaded*) Mr Packer.

"No, it's not possible," came the uncompromising reply.

"Can you at least tell me where we might get something?"

The restaurateur shrugged. "There is a little café opposite. You could try there."

Highly disgruntled, the party left, walked over the road and knocked on the café door which announced it was closed. Up went the bedroom window.

"Yes, what is it?" called down a lady. Mr Packer explained the situation.

"Right," the lady said. "I'll be right down." Wearing a dressing gown she ushered the party into her unpretentious dining room. Rousing her husband, they set about producing a simple meal, after which Mr Packer asked for the bill.

"Twenty pounds please sir." (This was several years ago.) A cheque was duly written out, folded in half and given to the lady.

"I want you to have this for the kindness you've shown me and my guests," said Mr Packer. "But there is one condition. Before you cash the cheque I want you to show it to the owner of the establishment over the road and tell him this is what one gets for good service." The cheque was for twenty *thousand* pounds.

Our toasted sandwich ladies didn't leave us as much as a fivepenny tip. Not that we expected it of course.

Smoking was allowed in all our rooms when we took over and after much huffing and puffing (that wasn't intended as a pun) we decided to take the decision to ban smoking in the dining rooms, but to allow it in the Snug bar.

And did this cause problems! How aggressive can smokers be when denied a puff! We removed ashtrays from the tables and put up discreet signs on the blackboard and on the menus. Too discreet for some.

One of the girls came to me. "Flick, lady on table one is smoking." Out I went.

"I'm terribly sorry, madam, but we no longer allow smoking in here." Giving me a steely glare madam stubbed her cigarette out on the tablemat. "I'll never come here again," she said, stabbing viciously. However much one would like to, one can't say: "Good!"

On being told she couldn't smoke at the table, a local doctor (who's long since left the district) departed, taking her bottle of wine with her saying: "I'm sorry we'll have to leave. I can't eat if I can't smoke with the meal."

At least she wasn't unpleasant about it, unlike Rob's ex-colonial. This time it was my husband's turn to deal with an over-heated smoker.

The gentleman arrived with two ladies in tow. On Rob's greeting him at the door, he barked: "Mary here?" a greeting we were to suffer many times. (People even walked out on hearing Mary had moved on, a great morale booster!) The gentleman and party were seated at table one and he lit up.

Rob smiled sweetly. "Sorry to get lunch off to a potentially bad start, but I'm afraid you can't smoke in here."

Much snorting into a pink gin. "Right. Give me an ashtray and I'll put the cigarette out. But I'll tell you this, sir, I'll never come here again after today."

"Well, *sir*, perhaps if you feel like that you might like to leave and have lunch elsewhere?"

"No, no, now we're here we'll stay. Give me a menu."

Lunch proceeded in its usual fashion, then our three colonials decided to take coffee in the Snug. Rob took it in for them.

The chap stood towering over Rob, hands behind back, gently rocking on his heels. "Well, young man (those were the days), we had a first class lunch, I'll give you that, but as I said, we'll never come again. We don't fly British Caledonian for the same bloody stupid reason."

In those days our no-smoking policy was the exception rather than the rule, but as time passed it was no longer remarked upon. Now it seems as though all restaurants must be non-smoking.

STANDARDS, HIGH, AND LOW

In the early days we were making a reasonable amount of money and before we moved up-market and took long-haul holidays, we would as a special treat stay at the Connaught Hotel for a few days. This, of course, is the Connaught in Carlos Place, London. From a professional point of view it was interesting to watch the perfect running of the dining room. I would have liked to have brought all the staff to lunch just to see how it should be done — although, to be fair to the youngsters, they always did a first class job and to serve like a Connaught waiter would have been somewhat over the top! But our lads and lasses were always friendly and obliging, which made up for any shortcomings in clearing away the plates.

The standards at the Connaught are extremely high and rightly so in my view. One evening, waiting to meet someone in the foyer, we noticed a young man and his girl friend attempt to get into the dining room, but Sir was refused, very politely, because he was not wearing a tie. Sir promptly threw a wobbly. "Do you know how much this suit cost?" he said. "It would look ridiculous to wear a tie."

"Nevertheless Sir, we cannot allow you in without a tie. If you ask the concierge he will provide you with one."

At which point our friend arrived and we left. This same friend, who came with us into the American Bar was refused entrance, as *he* had no tie. I must say his borrowed one with a polo-neck sweater looked ridiculous.

Even Rob on entering the library after dinner when taking off his jacket was very quietly and politely requested to put it back on.

In those days Colin was on the beat and he was asked to do some plain-clothes work. We were preparing to go out when we were paged to go to the lobby where someone was waiting for us. There, standing in these hallowed portals was our son dressed in a very scruffy tee-shirt and none-too-clean jeans. Accompanying him was an extremely smart uniformed WPC, the current girl friend. We had a short conversation about where we were going to meet later on; they went on their way, and we thought nothing more of it until we came to check out.

"Was everything all right?" we were asked.

"Of course," we replied.

"You had no problems during your stay with us?"

"No, none at all. Why do you ask?"

"We happened to notice yesterday morning that you were talking to the police."

We assume they thought that Colin was a mugger and that we were being asked to identify him. We soon put them straight!

In the days when my sight was beginning to fade I would frequently forget my specs; this I did one night at dinner so I couldn't read the amazing menu. On seeing my predicament the waiter produced a box of cheap specs for me to choose a pair. I was very impressed; this was probably the night I caused a bit of a problem. The head waiter, with fluent English of course, took the orders, but the other waiters were often foreign so didn't always understand what was said to them. I had ordered quail and when it arrived it had, quite correctly, its feet displayed. Now I'm not too keen on dead feet on my plate — picky, I know — so I asked for them to be removed. Nobody understood this request which caused so much consternation and confusion that I put up with the feet!

Similar, I suppose, to people coming to Mary's and asking for their slip soles to be filleted. Now I was very happy to do this for anyone who had failing vision or who was old and couldn't cope with the bones, but for young able-bodied customers I did feel it was an affectation, and much muttering went on in the kitchen, especially when the incident happened during a busy lunch. And the young lady topped it all by screaming: "I couldn't possibly eat these. They're full of roe! " *Well!*

As time went by we became more sure of ourselves. The business was ours, people came to see us and liked the way we did things. We even began to enjoy running the show, slowly changing things to our way of thinking.

We had confidence in our staff and they in us, so instead of closing for two weeks' holiday we decided to stay open with the senior girls and boys running the show, with a little help from a member of our family. January and February were always quiet on the Suffolk coast and we were open only for weekends, so we felt happy enough to leave them to it. On our return we sometimes found that there had been a hiccup and that there were one or two problems to iron out, but on the whole we felt that a little aggravation was worth enduring for a three-week break. Time enough to recharge the batteries.

Felicity supervises the new bed
in Zanzibar

Rob

Felicity

Gem

Gill, Di and Barbara. Press Ganged Christmas Staff

The big dining-room

TODAYS
ALTERNATIVES

REFERENDUM SOUP
GREEN HOPEFUL
FLAN
LABOUR FUDGE PIE
LIBERAL WAFFLES
TORY TRIFLE
WELSH RARITY
!———!

"Mary's" Election Day Menu!

The Little dining-room

Staff Party at Wenhaston. Max, Jason, Mel, Michael, Dawn, Patricia and Gem hiding.

BURGLARIES AND BREAK-INS

What made us change from holidays with friends and trips to London, to three weeks in an exotic location? The answer: a very salutary lesson on how transient life is, how it can be snuffed out in a moment of unexpected tragedy. I now firmly believe life should be lived to the full while one is able.

When my mother was still alive she always came to lunch on a Friday, Rob driving the six miles to Halesworth to fetch her. This particular Friday I had left something at home in Wenhaston and had asked Rob to pick it up for me on his way to get mother. I am quite sure he would have said "It will be a pleasure" not "Can't you remember anything?"

Time passed, no Rob. Lunch began and still no sign of him. This was unheard of, as he was very particular about being around to see people in and to seat them; also he liked to check that the meals looked presentable before they went into the dining room. I was beginning to worry when the phone rang – it was for me. A woman's voice said: "Hello? Mrs Jelliff?"

"Yes." I fidgeted; I needed to be in the kitchen.

"You don't know me; I am ringing you to say that your husband's been delayed, but that he's all right."

Thoroughly alarmed by this, I demanded: "What do you mean? Has he had an accident?"

"I can't say, but he's all right."

"What do you mean you can't say? You must tell me what's happened." I was getting cross, visions of car accidents, heart attacks, even that he had run off with another woman.

"I'll ring you back," the voice said and the line went dead.

I returned to the kitchen in no fit state to cope with lunchtime meat and two veg. Luckily I had help that day: Gerry was coping well. The staff were as concerned as I, but none of us could guess what had happened. Then the phone rang again; I rushed to pick it up. It was the strange woman.

"Mrs Jelliff, I'm sorry to have been so vague before, but your husband told me not to tell you what had happened, as he didn't want to worry you." Worry? I was frantic!

"Well — what has happened?"

"It seems that when he drove back to your house he disturbed two burglars. They ran off and he chased them. When they reached the common they attacked him. The police are here and the ambulance is on its way."

What she didn't tell me then was that the men had set about him with a jemmy and a chisel. Somehow Rob had staggered to a week-end cottage where the owner of the telephone voice was staying (coincidently she was called Mary.) At his request she rang the police and me.

Later she told me that she had just arrived for a weekend break and had opened the door to an apparition covered in blood. She insisted that he come in and lie down, but he said no, he would make a mess.

"I'm a nurse," she had said sternly, "and I can see that you're in no fit state to stand around." The note of authority worked, Rob meekly walked in and sat down. What she didn't say was that she had only done a week's training with the Red Cross.

Now all I wanted to do was to get back home and see him. I had no car and still had lunch to cook. Everyone rallied round. Gerry said that he could manage lunch and Mel said she would drive me home, as there were enough staff on to manage without her. If there were any hold-ups they would just explain what had happened.

What *had* happened? I wish I knew!

Not wishing to upset my mother I quickly phoned her and told her that there had been a slight mishap and that Rob couldn't get over. Then we were off.

Mel was very calm and matter-of-fact. She told me not to worry, that if Rob had a head wound there might be a lot of blood but it would look worse than it was. On approaching the house the road was cordoned off by the police. I leapt out of the car and said to the nearest policeman: "I'm the lady of the house. Where's my husband?" What a silly thing to say!

He took me to the cottage where Rob was. What a poor soul he looked. He could hardly stand and his Barbour was covered in blood. I put my arms around him.

"What have they done to you?" I cried.

The paramedics were bustling around, anxious to get him to hospital. We managed a quick hug and he was whisked away, through red lights, bells ringing, the lot. Or so he told me, eighteen stitches in the head later.

The police had wanted me to stay behind to show them around the house.

"Is it in a terrible mess?" I asked. They were non-committal but told me to be prepared for the worst. I hadn't realised that they hadn't been able to get into the house as the door was still locked. The thieves had tried to jemmy it open with no success – it still bears the scars today. They had had more luck with a sitting room window and this was how they had got in. In fact the house was quite tidy, the thieves being professionals rather than vandals. As if that was any consolation!

I suppose they might have been going to turn it over but Rob had disturbed them. It's all a bit hazy as to what happened next. I know Mel went back to the restaurant and at police insistence I phoned a friend and asked her to come and hold my hand; perhaps the police thought I might succumb to hysteria if left on my own. So

I rang Colin. He was now in the Met and his sergeant very kindly gave him compassionate leave so he was home within three hours. He phoned our daughter Pennie who came home the next day.

Not a lot was stolen, but several bits of silver had been taken out of our extremely well hidden hidey-hole and were stacked up ready to go. Even the police said that it would have been unlikely to have been found without inside knowledge. We'd recently had builders in, local men as honest as the day is long, but they had subcontracted some of the work to not-so-local men who possibly weren't so honest.

Rob was out of hospital that evening with Colin looking after him, as I had to return to the restaurant to do dinner. I remember dropping a dish of chicken on the floor and wailing: "I shouldn't even *be* here; I should be at home nursing my husband."

No doubt if Patricia had been in the kitchen with me she would have told me to pull myself together, and quite right too! As it was, Kathryn was with me and she calmly cleared up after me and got on with things.

As is Sod's Law it was an extremely busy weekend. Rob — bless him — staggered in to work on the Sunday. At the end of trading we sat and counted all the pennies, then went home. Sitting quietly that evening I had a sudden thought. "Rob, did we put the money in the safe?" We drove back at breakneck speed to find the money sitting innocently on the table!

The following weekend we were burgled at Mary's. We felt quite paranoid. However, this was an amateur job. Several shops in the village were also broken into and petty cash taken: we hadn't been singled out, unlike with the burglary at home. That, we later learned, was done by a gang working the area – they targeted business people going to work all day and not returning until the evening. A horrid feeling to think that one's comings and goings had been clocked with evil intent. The thieves were not caught for our job although Rob had ID'd the men. They had, of course, got an alibi for the time in question.

Sometime later when Colin had injured himself, or rather a drug dealer had injured him while resisting arrest, he was recuperating in a police nursing home where he met a sergeant who had some knowledge of our case. The sergeant told Colin that the men had been caught for some other burglary and were behind bars. It was some little consolation.

We suffered yet another break-in at 'Mary's' later that year. This time we were staying over and the spaniels were asleep upstairs. We always said that they had put their paws over their ears and swore that they had heard nothing! By this time, of course, we were a bit sharper: there was nothing of value to take, just a bottle of whisky and the inconvenience of a broken window.

How easily I could have lost Rob, if the blows to his head had been lower or harder. It doesn't bear thinking about. It was this which brought home to us how transient life is. With this in mind and a cheque for criminal injuries incurred, I asked Rob: "Where in the world would you like to go for a holiday? I think we should grab opportunities as they come so in our old age we don't sit and say 'If only…' " Surprisingly, Rob agreed. We spent many pleasurable hours poring over brochures and settled on the Seychelles, somewhere Rob had always wanted to go. At that time I don't think I had even heard of them.

What a wonderful holiday it was, even if I was nearly drowned by a strong wave! But that's another story. We were hooked. A few days at the Connaught Hotel is a treat and cheaper than a long-haul holiday, but there was no comparison. From then on we enjoyed an exotic holiday every year. The memories we have are worth every penny that we spent. Diving off the Maldives, stepping over iguanas in the Galapagos, watching turtles laying their eggs on a beach in Borneo — the list is legion.

Most of our customers were pleased for us. "You work so hard you deserve a break," they said and seemed quite happy to be bored by our little anecdotes. On the other hand some customers were peeved that we weren't there to look after them should they deign to visit our restaurant. A few even stopped coming, but they were in the minority.

MANOR HOUSE MUSHROOMS

Button mushrooms
Small carton cream cheese
1oz butter
Parsley, Chives, Garlic
Seasoning
Coating batter
Seasoned flour
Deep fat

METHOD

Wipe and de-stalk mushrooms. Beat cheese, then slowly add melted butter. Chop herbs and crush garlic. Add to cheese and season. Fill the middle of the mushrooms with the mixture. Toss mushrooms in seasoned flour. Dip into coating batter. Very carefully place in hot oil, 190°C. Turn when golden brown and drain. Serve with a small salad garnish.

RUSSIAN MUSHROOMS

½lb button mushrooms
Seasoned flour
Butter
Double cream

METHOD

Cut mushrooms into quarters unless they are very small, then leave whole or cut in half. Toss in seasoned flour. Melt butter. Sauté mushrooms off. Gently add the cream, until the mushrooms are sitting in a luscious sauce. Check seasoning. Serve at once in a warmed ramekin or place in a dish and warm through in oven when needed. Top with chopped parsley.

MANOR HOUSE SMOKIES

½ lb smoked fish
Milk
½ pint cheese sauce
Grated cheese and breadcrumbs

METHOD

Poach smoked fish in milk. Use the milk in which the fish has been cooked in the cheese sauce. Place a little sauce in the base of a ramekin dish. Flake some of the fish on top. Cover with the cheese sauce. Repeat in several ramekins. Top with grated cheese mixed with breadcrumbs. Place in hot oven 200°C for 15-20 minutes. Garnish with sprig of parsley.

BAKED BANANA AND STILTON

1 small banana
Ends of stilton
A little cream

METHOD

Mash banana and place in a heat proof scallop dish, top with crumbled stilton. Add a little cream. Place in microwave for 1.5-2 minutes to soften. Put under hot grill. Garnish with the inevitable sprig of parsley. Serve with thinly sliced bread and butter.

There was usually only one cook in the kitchen, two on busy days, so there was no time for fancy garnishing. Every morning someone chopped parsley, sprigged parsley, cut lemon wedges and melted some butter to glaze the vegetables before they went out. These were all placed on the serving top and the girls and boys garnished as appropriate. Oh, I mustn't forget the damp cloth to wipe up the dribbles the cooks might have incurred in their haste to get the meal out.

TRAITS AND TRIALS

I n the winter we employed between five and six members of staff, and in the summer the number fluctuated to as many as thirty. *We were responsible for a payroll of thirty!* Not all full time I hasten to add. The winter staff were the hardcore and the summer staff were mostly youngsters and college students. Without studying psychology or any other -ology it became apparent that the more academically able the person the more lacking in common sense he (or she) was, with absolutely no feeling of urgency even when dockets were knee high and customers were queuing at the doors. This would send Rob to screaming point and on one famous frantic moment he was heard to shout to one of my girls: "My God, you're as thick as your sister!"

No doubt this lass (and her sister?) is scarred for life. It is a good job that the present employment legislation was not in place then as I'm sure we would have spent the greater part of our lives in Court. I had my moments as well. Patricia would say: "When Felicity stamps her foot, look out." It was a foible I didn't know I had.

I remember showing the girls a holiday snap when there had been a hiccup at our hotel and I was supervising the placing of a new bed in our room. (It was in Zanzibar.) They laughed: "We recognise that posture," one said. "I bet you were giving them hell!" And I had always thought I was the soul of reasonableness and good temper.

Before the alterations were done to the building, the kitchen window overlooked the doors of the outside loos. I stood at the sink by the window clearing up after a day's trading when I espied a youngster who had obviously been told to clean the loos, not a popular job. He stood vaguely looking about, slowly sweeping the floor. I opened the window and shouted: "For goodness sake, John, put a bit more effort into it." Then I was called from the kitchen. As I left I heard Jo shout: "What Flick really means is get your finger out and your bloody arse into gear." Succinctly put!

Situations could arise out of nothing and whereby in industry no doubt there is a personnel officer to help sort out problems, in a busy restaurant where customers are waiting to be served, counselling isn't very high on the agenda. We became aware something was wrong when a hysterical woman came to the window saying she had been given the wrong order and our waitress had got an attitude problem. Unusual, as our girls were always very pleasant. We tried to placate the woman by changing her order, but she wasn't having any.

"All I wanted was a cream tea," she said and retired in tears to the lawn.

Where was the offending waitress? I found her in what we euphemistically called the staff room. She too was in floods of tears.

"I took the order out and I know I got it right, but that woman insisted it was all wrong. She was very unkind. I'm no good at this job. I think I'll go home."

Now in fact she was a very capable waitress and we had a busy afternoon ahead, so in spite of orders piling up, time had to be taken out to soothe the girl and tell her all was well. The woman on the lawn I left to her husband.

People can be unkind without thinking. One lass, on taking a tray into the garden, tripped and dropped the lot. Everyone laughed uproariously and none offered to help. Of course she dissolved into tears. On this occasion Rob consoled her and helped her clear up the mess. I am sure it is apocryphal that he read a lecture to the assembled customers about being unfeeling and uncaring.

Sometimes we would be caught out. We could be working with a winter staff, the sun would shine and the world could descend on us. Nightmare stuff. I think we all had sense-of-humour failures on such days. We would dash about, heads down, pretending we couldn't see the people at the back door waiting to eat in the garden.

STAYING POWERS

Staff would stay for varying lengths of time. The longest was for our entire thirteen years and the shortest was for two hours.

It seemed when people came for interviews the old stagers would weigh them up and take bets as to how long they would last. I think the two-hour stint took us all by surprise! She was a pleasant girl, had had waitress experience and lived in the village. Ideal we thought. All seemed to be going well and she seemed happy enough. Suddenly she said: "I think I need to change my skirt." Abruptly she left, never to be seen again.

Another short stay was for two and a half days. The young lady in question decided on her third day she would go home for lunch, but, she said, she would return. At the appointed hour we looked for her but there was no sign, nor the next day. Finally I rang her home; her mother answered the telephone.

"I was wondering what had happened to Naomi," I asked.

"Oh," said mother. "I'm afraid she's had a nervous breakdown."

ALL WASHED UP

A good washer-up is an absolute godsend and we employed many of different degrees and backgrounds. An unfulfilled chef, an ex-policeman, a vicar, a stray Israeli, a retired postman, not to mention the unrequited composer.

We inherited Malcolm. Although he was our washer-up and gofer his dream was to become a chef. To this end he went once a week to catering college. Occasionally I would let him help in the kitchen but he wasn't one hundred percent reliable. Every so often he seemed to have a blip and wander off. Just before he left us to take on a job that involved more cooking, he said that he would like to cook a Chinese meal for Rob and me and some other members of staff. As he seemed so keen we thanked him and arranged for him to use the kitchen at Mary's and we would eat in the dining room. The appointed hour came and went and no Malcolm. "Another of his Walter Mitty dreams," someone said, when in he came with his mother, and lots of pots and pans. In his defence I have to say it was one of the best Chinese meals I have ever tasted.

The composer was one of the four members of staff whom we had to sack. He was over six-foot tall and very thin. He would stand staring into space, no doubt composing his latest work. He seemed to be quite oblivious to the washing-up piling up around him. Finally we would try to goad him into action, then he might scrape into the bin the detritus that returned on the plates — or he might *eat* it. He had one run-in with Mel, which was the final straw. She was disgusted to see him standing still, as was his wont, but picking his nose. *In a restaurant!* Naturally she remonstrated with him. Looking down from his lofty height to her five foot something, he said: "I don't know why you're so worried about a minor thing like that when we could all be zapped by Sizewell tomorrow." (The nuclear power stations are less than ten miles away.)

Be that as it may, he had to go.

Then there was Patricia. She joined us and worked like a little fury, but she was destined for greater things, as you will see.

Mika our Israeli appeared as if from out of nowhere. There was so much crashing about in the sink while he was with us, but he got the job done. On helping at an 'outside do' taking place at a local village hall he saw an honesty box where one placed money to pay for the electricity used. He was quite amazed. He said that in Israel not only would people not put money in the box, but if anyone was foolish to do so someone else would steal it!

When not washing-up, he made intricate silver jewellery for us which we sold for him in our little craft shop. When he left he gave me a pair of earrings as I had been so kind to him. My children were rather rude about them: "Mother, why are you wearing silver cannabis leaves in your ears?" they asked. I hadn't realised that's what they were – I wore them anyway.

A good-looking lad, Michael was with us for three years while he was trying for university. He was a great asset as after a while he could dive into the kitchen and fry me some fish and chips while I did something more intricate, but I don't think he ever forgave me for telling him that on Patricia's day off I wanted him to do the fish and chips for a forty-seater coach party, only telling him at the last minute I was teasing him. He could have been a good chef but he decided that an arts degree was for him.

Two brothers from the village often helped out. They were always most obliging; I could pick up the phone and one or other would come at a moment's notice and help out if he possibly could.

Then came Roger. He had retired from being a postman in Peckham. His family had had holidays in Southwold for years and had always dreamed of living there. Roger was offered early retirement and a cottage came available at about the same time so he jumped at the chance of living by the sea. Roger lightened our lives considerably. Sunday was one of his days, the busiest and most fraught of the week. He would sidle up to me in a conspiratorial manner and tell me the most appalling jokes – worse even than cracker jokes, but they appealed to my sense of humour and got lunch off to a good start. One such joke was:

"I went into a pub and asked for a packet of helicopter-flavoured crisps. The landlord said he was sorry but he only had plain (plane?)." "I asked why he didn't have helicopter crisps and he said it was because they hadn't taken off."

And this one: "Irish police announced today they'd found the body of a horse with a bullet hole in its forehead. They think it may be the missing horse Shergar but, while keeping an open mind, they are ruling out suicide."

I once complained to one of my girls that no one ever laughed at my jokes. She looked me straight in the eye and said: "That's because they're so bad, Flick!"

Roger's jokes were bad but he obviously had a knack of telling them as there was never a stony silence after *he* delivered the punch line.

His jokes were to bring about an amazing coincidence (one of many that we were to experience). It was just before we retired. Roger told us a particularly bad joke which had made even Rob laugh so much that he repeated it to some customers who had been coming to Mary's for years.

After telling the joke Rob said, "That was from our washer-up, Roger. He came from Peckham."

"Really," said the customer. "He wasn't a postman, was he?"

"Yes, he was."

"Is his surname Douglas?"

Intrigued, Rob said: "Yes, it is."

"I don't believe it!" cried the customer. "He's my cousin. I

45

heard that he had moved down this way, but I haven't seen him for years. "Of course we pulled Roger away from the sink and reunited him.

What all my washer-uppers hated — and who can blame them — was cleaning our rather ancient fish fryers. I have done my share of that task and it's not to be recommended. In an over-zealous moment I put oven cleaner on all the ovens and put the fryers to soak expecting the then washer-up to cope with them the next day. He must have guessed as he rang in sick. Guess who got the job!

CLEANERS AND CLEANER

Cleaning is another job that isn't at all popular, nevertheless it is very important. Shirley was with us for our early years, keeping the dining-rooms spotless. She left us to look after her handicapped son and we were sorry to see her go as she was reliable and thorough. Then came Mel's mum, another of the old school. Unfortunately she suffered a nasty accident while cleaning a passage-way and somehow a heater fell on her leg. Bless her, she was far more concerned about finishing her work than her own plight.

Another cleaner needed to be found. As the youngsters were so bad at cleaning the loos and mopping the floors, skipping them when they could, we decided to add these chores to the cleaner's spec. A young man applied for the job and got it. He did an excellent job and took a pride in what he did, coming to work very early in the morning in his little van with his sweet little dog. He was usually finishing as Rob and I arrived. He and Patricia seemed to get on very well and if I wanted to make a request or to give a slight criticism I would ask her to pass it on, as one summer he appeared in the briefest shorts I have ever seen. Possibly I thought these weren't quite the thing for a genteel tea-room so I got Patricia to suggest that he might wear something a bit more substantial. Sometimes I did feel that he wasn't quite of this world. If our current washer-upper let us down I would ask him if he would stay on and help. He could never give me a straight answer but would have to go and sit in his van and think about it. Sometimes he would oblige but sometimes he would just drive away in silence. He left us because he felt we didn't appreciate him – totally untrue.

After this, several people came and went with varying degrees of success. A glamorous young woman from the village; Patricia and Mel in the winter; even Roger and his daughter had a go at the job.

CHEFS COME AND GO

To get hold of a good reliable cook or chef is nigh impossible. Pauline, who helped us out in our early days was a good cook; she worked hard and had our interests at heart. In the summer she loved to serve on the back door, and very proficient she was too, helping the youngsters with cakes to speed service into the garden. However Suffolk proved too quiet for her and after two years she returned to Yorkshire.

Gerry was with us for a short while. He had had his own café, but had sold on and was waiting for another career move. He turned up again much later in our lives as a personnel officer or some such for youngsters on some government scheme and we took on one of his charges.

By the time Pauline left, Jo had become proficient in the kitchen and could run it with help, so occasionally I would go into the hot seat. The beginning of the slippery slope! Jo and I worked well together, but as with all young things she got married and moved away.

Kathryn came to help in our early days to back up cook on a Friday and Saturday evening. She and Pauline didn't get on terribly well, being like chalk and cheese. Pauline was larger than life, blonde and quite a big girl, Kathryn was (and still is) extremely slim, dark and quite reserved. Kathryn stayed with us for many years and supplied us with many of our cakes including our popular lemon cake, but on one delivery when she opened the tin she was mortified to see that her husband Fred had taken a large slice out of a cake. She wasn't very happy whenever an order for Manor House Mushrooms came up. There would be a loud sigh from her corner and a black cloud would descend.

When whoever was number one cook at the time had a day off, Cara would come in to cover. She and her husband ran an outside catering business and then took a delicatessen. It soon became obvious that working for us as well as running her own business was proving too much, so with regret she left us although in an emergency she would still help out.

For a while we employed two rather large young men, who seemed to take up an awful lot of space. David was the number two chef so it fell to his lot to make the daily batches of scones and doughnuts, which he absolutely hated. Consequently they were made at break-neck speed with an incredible amount of mess. Flour everywhere – on the work surfaces, on the floor, probably on the ceilings, then from the floor onto his shoes so it got trodden all over the kitchen. He had been in the army and found working with a mainly female staff very difficult, especially as he had me in charge. He never called me by name, but always referred to me as Boss. He was quite an imaginative cook and it was he who came up with our Manor House Mushrooms, an extremely popular starter with the customers although extremely unpopular with Kathryn.

Both our young men left us under rather unfortunate circumstances, so there we were about to start a summer season and no cook. Patricia tentatively told us she had been an assistant cook in a previous life so would be happy to back up. I took the plunge and agreed rather half-heartedly that I would take on the number one slot. And there I was in the kitchen, never to be released.

Patricia and I worked together for about nine years and on the whole got on pretty well together. We would both have funny turns, but luckily they never coincided. She had the curious gift of anticipating what I needed, and she would also stop me needling Rob when I felt particularly bolshie. Of course we had our little disasters, kept between the two of us, and we would quickly improvise our way out. For instance, if a meal was slow coming out and Rob was feeling particularly brave, he would put his head round the corner and ask: "Everything alright, girls?"

"Fine," we would say, "absolutely fine." And then we would panic!

What really upset us was when orders went up thick and fast and no questions were asked as to how the various dishes were holding up. Being freshly-made they weren't finite so if there was a

Mrs. J with pistol at the ready

49

run on a particular dish it could run out. "Four lamb left," we would say. Two orders would go up, total five lamb. Result, a shouting match. All good fun.

On one occasion five dockets down, a table of six went up. They all wanted plaice. Was there enough? We did a hurried count: no, only enough for five. However, when we got to the relevant order we found we had miscounted and there was enough for six. So we sent it out. Were the customers grateful? No. Two days later we received a letter complaining that the person who had had the plaice that we had 'found' had been ill. We were lucky not to have a visit from the dreaded EHO.

On Pat's day off, Lou would come in to help. Whenever she was in the kitchen there was a run on sausages, quite incredibly. She did have one bad habit, however. In the middle of getting a meal out she would suddenly remember some anecdote and she would stop everything until she had told me the tale. Rather frustrating.

In our last year or so I 'did' dinners on my own with one of the girls dashing in to help at crucial moments. Although we did cook more adventurous dishes in the evenings we kept on the faithful plaice and chips. To make drambuie steak look presentable and fry fish and chips at the same time was quite a problem. "Help!" I would shout and someone would oblige. If we were relatively quiet we couldn't justify asking a washer-up to come in so I would face my many pots and pans on my own. Daunting!

Rob would come in all smiles, "Well done. By the way, table five would like a word."

I can tell you the last thing one wants to do after a busy session is to go out into the dining room to 'have a word'.

When Patricia was in she would say, "Off you go. I'll do the washing-up."

So off would come the apron and into the dining room I would trot and swan about making polite conversation — and secretly enjoying every minute of it. No second bidding!

WAITERS AND WAITRESSES

The waiting-on staff were mostly youngsters with not much experience of what was expected of them and they would try the patience of our older, more experienced girls. We gave them all some training but even so we still slipped up. One lass told us she had had a lot of waitressing experience. Foolishly we didn't follow up her references. On her first day I was standing beside her while she made up a tray for a coffee. I casually ran my eye over her tray – after all, it was only one coffee.

"Don't forget the saucer," I said walking into the dining room.

I stood talking to a customer while watching our lass put the cup in front of her lady, and the saucer on the table beside it. At least she took it off the tray which is more than some did.
Thank you burger emporiums – you have a lot to answer for!

I *did* learn to take nothing for granted. Things that are second nature to my generation are no longer *de rigeur* to this. As an example, we tried to instil into the young the necessity of being aware of what was happening in the dining-room as a whole and not to have tunnel vision. When the staff had finished serving a table they should look around to see if anyone else needed anything or to see if any tables needed clearing, and when clearing a table we insisted the waiter took a damp cloth to wipe down the surface so it looked presentable for the next customer.

I was showing one young man how we liked our sandwiches presented: bread cut into four triangles, two standing up and one lying down on each side, a piece of cucumber and tomato on the lying-down sandwiches, a wisp of cress scattered over the whole, finishing off with a few crisps on the plate.

"There," I said. "You can now prepare a sandwich. Now *you* make the ham sandwich and before you take it out show it to me." It was just as well I took that precaution because our young man came proudly up to me with: "Please check my sandwich."

"Of course." I looked it over – perfect. "That's absolutely fine . Just one small thing – where's the ham?"

The poor chap was totally deflated.

This exercise came after another experience. It was a very busy lunch and Patricia and I were up to our eyeballs when a voice said tentatively: "I've got an order for an egg sandwich."

I looked up. It was a new girl but she seemed to be sensible. "Could you make it?"

"Yes, but where is the bread?"

I told her. She went off, but a little later she was back. "Where's the butter?"

I told her. Off she went, then back she came again. "Where's the mayonnaise?"

I told her. She went again, only to return.

"I can't find the eggs."

I was a little fraught at this point. Seeing a pan at the back of the stove with eggs in, I assumed (another thing – never assume) Patricia had cooked them earlier that morning. "Here you are," I probably snarled.

A moment later she was back. "Don't you cook your eggs for an egg sandwich?"

Patricia told me later that she had meant to boil the eggs but had forgotten.

I have a feeling this might have been the young lady who had the nervous breakdown. If not, probably it should have been.

Rob occasionally helped with staff training, not always successfully. One Sunday afternoon he took a new member under his wing to show him how to prepare an elementary tray for the garden, one tea, and one coffee. The tray was checked to see if it was clean. It was pointed out that things should be taken in sequence: cups, saucers, teaspoons, as it was for outside; packets of white and brown sugar were put in a bowl,lastly the coffee filter, and a jigger (small container of cream) placed on the lid of the filter to stop it blowing off; a teapot with teabags, a hot water jug, milk in a milk jug. They were carefully filled from the still. Then the tray was taken out to the garden, the name of the customer called and acknowledged.

"There," said Rob. " I did that myself so if you have a complaint you know where to come."

One minute later the customer was back. No water had been poured on the coffee filter. There was much merriment all round.

Patricia spotted one youngster washing lettuce in hot water. Luckily she hadn't added washing-up liquid!

I walked out with one girl and watched while she laid the table from her tray when I spotted she had black nail varnish on. All nail varnish is taboo, but *black*! Yuk! Back in the kitchen she was very apologetic and used my nail varnish remover with good grace.

The girls, and even to some extent the boys, were told various rules about no nail varnish, hair tied back, no excessive jewellery. No doubt this sounds starchy and stuffy but is necessary for food hygiene.

We also had to show the youngsters how to lay a table. They had to check that the table was clean, that the mat was clean, that the cutlery was shiny and the knives pointing the same way towards the mat. We were finding that youngsters had less and less idea how to lay a table as the years went by. If given half a chance they would put the tray on the table and let the customer get on with it. For outside this was fine but *in the restaurant?*

Most of the staff got on well with each other but inevitably there would be personality clashes. With judicious rota planning I could make sure they were on different shifts so that there was no bad atmosphere in the dining room.

One summer we had an exceptionally pretty group of girls on the team and at the end of the season they organised a trip to Yarmouth to a nightclub. We were asked if we would like to join them. Our initial reaction was: 'No, thank you very much,' but on reflection we thought: it was a compliment to be asked. We were 'management' and should show our faces.

We hadn't been to Yarmouth for years, not since before we were married when we had enjoyed the night life of the town.

And so off we went. Joining our bevy of beauties at a dimly lit table, we sat down. The evening progressed and the girls left us to dance. Rob went off to the bar to get some drinks. I sat minding my own business when I was joined by a young man who proceeded to chat me up. It *was* pretty dark! I must have made a hit as after a while he said: "It's a bit dead here. Let's go on to Rosie's." At this point Rob arrived with our drinks and my young man left hurriedly. But Rob had done equally well; while waiting to be served, a large lorry driver with bulging biceps and tattoos had taken a fancy to Rob and tried to entice him outside!

After all this excitement we decided it was time to leave. We would relive our past and walk down the prom to look at the lights and eat a hot dog. How times have changed — the dog was quite disgusting: a dry bun, a lukewarm sausage and tinned onions. Yuk! It transpired the next morning that the only people who had 'pulled' that evening were Rob and me!

Some of the youngsters stayed with us for several years. We became quite fond of them and became quite involved in their lives: worrying about exam results, grieving with them when love affairs went wrong, being a shoulder to cry on when parents split up. A white-faced child would come in, not able to talk about the problem for weeks, and then it would all spill out.

Mostly these dramas happened at very busy times. When Colin and Corrina's relationship was ending, first one of them came down for consolation or to let off steam and then the other would want a word. All the while I was trying to organise dinner, one beef, no veg, and croquettes, or one side salad, no pots. No doubt I was not as sympathetic as I might have been.

One Christmas a new girlfriend of Colin's, came to stay for the holiday but on New Year's Day they had a grand falling out. We were very busy doing our Victorian Breakfast, knee deep in porridge, smoked fish and bacon. While the girlfriend sat outside in tears in the car, Colin, white-faced and silent, sat in the Snug. Pennie rushed between the two of them trying to patch things up to no avail, instead of concentrating on her waitressing job.

Oh, the joys of young love!

As far as I know there were no romantic attachments formed between the young staff. One young lady was quite smitten with one of our good-looking lads. He was quite unaware of this adulation and when she cycled miles to see him on his last day to say farewell he said casually: "Bye. Enjoy the rest of your life."

He didn't understand why we were all so horrified at his cruelty. "I didn't know," he protested. "I thought she'd come for her wages."

Roger certainly had a soft spot for a pretty girl. One of them, Leslie, a rather intense young lady he would tease unmercifully (in the nicest possible way I hasten to add). One day for whatever reason she had sprayed herself with Dettol. Roger thought this was wonderful and followed her about like a little dog!

Certainly the young kept one on one's toes. Dawn walked out into the dining room oblivious to the fact that one of the boys had placed a plastic snake on her shoulder as she passed by. It wasn't until she leaned forward to clear a table and it slid onto a customer's plate that she was aware of the reptile. Retribution took place on her return to the kitchen.

In spite of a hectic insight into the catering business, some of the youngsters have made it their career. Chefs no less, the most stressful job of all. Max had showed his enthusiasm early on, and had been allowed into our domain to put into practice some of his ideas. Matthew we thought was going on to do exciting things in the RAF. Perhaps it seemed tame after Sunday lunch at Mary's.

Quite recently Rob and I were having a quiet drink at a local hostelry. I needed to use the facilities and on my way back to our table a voice called out: "Hello, Sweetheart," or some such. Well, I thought, that can't be me, so I ignored the salutation. Sitting down I surreptitiously looked around to see who might be talking to whom. A tanned sun-glassed man was waving to me. Tentatively I waved back.

"I'll be over to see you in a moment," called the man.

"Who's that?" asked Rob.

"No idea," I murmured.

The man came over to our table and recognition began to dawn.

"I don't know whether to shake you by the hand or knock you down," said Matthew's father. "We thought our son was all set for a career in the R.A.F., but having worked at Mary's the only thing he wanted to do was to be a chef."

I really can't think why.

Justin – now *he* had kept quiet about his ambitions. It wasn't until some time after he left that we heard he had became a *commis* chef at a local hotel. And Mel left to work for a film and television catering firm.

One customer asked: "Felicity, why do you employ all these young men?"

I smiled sweetly (I hope it wasn't a leer) as one of these particularly good looking young men passed by, and I replied: "Now, why do you think?"

Did I hear her say: "Well, *really!*"?

Over our thirteen years I think we sacked only three or four people: the nose picker, a chef, and one young man who was a smasher. He was given many warnings that if he dropped one more glass he would have to pay for it out of his wages, but that still did no good so he had to go. He was also rather a troublemaker, sidling up and listening to conversations then passing on information embellished from a slanted point of view.

HOW TO SET AN EXAMPLE

I may have expected perfection from my staff, but I didn't live up to it myself. One busy Sunday I was ready with a meal and there was no one available to take it out. With bad humour I ripped off my pinny and took the plates to the table myself, mentally sorting out the next order.

The man sitting at the table looked up and said: "Cheer up. It might never happen."

"It just did," I snapped. "I'm out here."

Another time on taking out a tea tray I somehow managed to knock it on the back of a chair. The milk jug went up in the air, and turned upside down into a lady's lap.

For the first course of our Victorian Breakfast we served Buck's Fizz. One morning I took out a tray with four full glasses on it but on reaching the table first one glass fell over, followed by the other three. That's when I practiced being the boss, for one advantage of this is that one can retreat in confusion and send out a member of staff to clear up the mess. Customer relations just wasn't my strong point.

I took out a hot meal to a customer in the garden, a member of the local theatre company as it happens. I put down the main course in front of the man, then the beautifully prepared and served vegetables in their own dish. Then I watched as he picked up the vegetables and plonked them on top of the meat.

"Do you know," I said, "that I spend a lot of time thinking what vegetables look good together and arranging them accordingly, and you just throw them on your plate."

Somewhat taken aback he looked at me and then at his plate. "Well," he said, "I have to admit that was rather a crass thing to do."

Nor were my experiences at being helpful in the dining room always totally successful. A local lord came in to book a table for dinner. It was to be terribly hush-hush as one of his guests was someone of great importance and he was not to be named. Fine. I knew that short of him being the Prince of Wales I wouldn't recognise him, and I didn't. I still idly ponder who this person was and why he was in Walberswick incognito, the days of Christine Keeler being over. Anyway a sea trout was asked for and duly bought. The evening arrived and the request was made for me to go out and serve the trout at the table. Great! Off I went with not terribly good grace, smiles all round. "Good evening," and so on.

"I would like the pearl," said the unknown. Hunting for it in dim light I was not successful as he told me.

"Sorry," said I. "I've not got my specs on and can't see." Off I went to get them and all was revealed and the unknown had his 'pearl'. Our local fishmonger told us that the age of the fish can be seen by the rings on the pearl, the small nugget of flesh under the gill cover.

I discovered when I misread a docket I really needed to wear my spectacles, as I sent out four steaks instead of four soles. I still maintain it was Rob's fault for writing up the order in pencil, as was his wont, instead of the requested pen. From then on I wore half-lens specs.

When Pauline was with us I was able to slip out and do the occasional outside catering job. For many years I had 'done' the house party for Lord and Lady Gladwyn at Bramfield Hall, south of

Halesworth, and loved every minute of it. It was like living in a bygone world especially in the early days when I had a butler and a parlour maid of the old school working with me. I didn't mind in the least being the wrong side of the green baize door as being the cook I was top dog.

For several years Lady Diana Cooper was a house guest: Maggie Smith in *Gosforth Park* was exactly like her.

One little anecdote about Lady Diana.

At the very first dinner party I did at the Hall, I was asked to get her a vodka. I was young and very inexperienced but I trotted into the drawing room and poured a measure of vodka. What, I thought, goes with vodka? Oh yes, tonic. So I poured a small amount into a glass and took it to Lady Diana in the dining room. Graciously she thanked me, but as I slipped from the room an imperious voice exclaimed: "Somebody has put something *disgusting* in my vodka." I hadn't realized she drank her spirits neat.

After dinner she came into the kitchen. "A lovely meal, my dear," she said, "but you know I simply can't taste a thing." A somewhat backhanded compliment, which makes me wonder how she knew about the tonic.

Anyway, I returned on this particular weekend to the restaurant having done my select dinner for ten in fine fettle, even going out into the dining room and being nice! Rob is still amazed by the fact that when table six asked if there was any chance at all of them having Zabaglione I said "of course" and went, humming to myself, to the back kitchen. There I whisked and whisked until the pudding was made. "Wonderful!" The customers were enthralled, but went without leaving a tip. *Typical!*

Another happy occasion was when I congratulated two little children on eating up their large lunch. "You'll grow up into fine young men," I said. Not so, as they turned out to be girls.

Rob always wanted to give every customer what was requested, and rightly so I'm sure, but sometimes it is almost impossible. On and rightly so I'm sure, but sometimes it is almost impossible. On one famous occasion Jo and I had just finished an extremely busy lunch. I had sent Jo off for a quick break and I was starting the mammoth job of clearing the kitchen. Every surface was covered with used utensils and the sink was full of dirty washing-up. I had my back to the window, wiping down and tidying a bench, trying to get some semblance of order before we started high teas. I was feeling absolutely whacked, when from the window I heard my beloved's voice call out: "Any chance of sausage and chips in the garden?"

Thinking this must be his warped sense of humour and it was some sort of joke I didn't bother to turn but snarled: "You must be bloody joking!"

This was *in extremis* as, normally, I didn't swear, nor did I realise that the customer was standing next to Rob until I heard him say: "There. I did say it was unlikely"!

I doubt the customer ever came again.

Nor was I the best saleswoman in the world. A near neighbour tapped at the back door one Friday evening. "Tell me, Felicity," she said brightly. "Is there anything on the menu that will tempt me away from my television tonight?"

Now I know that I should have extolled the delights of my culinary prowess, but this remark put my back up and I felt sure that even if I went painstakingly through the menu she still wouldn't come.

"I shouldn't think so for a minute," I said. "I should stay at home." She did.

FINGERS IN THE TILL

We were lucky to have honest staff as only once was there a problem with the till. We had a shrewd idea whose fingers had gone in, as we were only short the day this person worked. As she was with us for a very short period we let the matter slide. But missing food was a problem that just had to be addressed. Every member of staff had to be told of the theft and they were very upset. It was all very unpleasant, and when we realised we couldn't solve it, we had to threaten to call in the police. And then the thieving stopped.

The staff kept their tips in a box in a cupboard under the stairs and people who had gone home before tips were sorted had their share put in a money bag. One summer there were murmurings that amounts of money were going missing. The youngsters thought they knew who was responsible but didn't confront the culprit, but I think enough hints were dropped for the person in question to desist.

Inland Revenue requested a Tronc Master which I think is a lovely title for the distributor of the tips. Patricia took over this role and did it very efficiently. There was no differential between the staff, from the newest recruit to the most experienced, all had equal shares, although I believe if one member of the team was particularly lazy he — or she — did get slightly less. Officially Rob and I knew nothing about the tipping system, but obviously one was slightly aware!

FISHERMAN'S POT

1/2 lb cooked white fish.

1/2 pint white sauce flavoured with lobster bisque.

Tin red salmon.

Prawns to personal taste.

1 lb potatoes, cooked.

Breadcrumbs and grated cheese.

METHOD

Mix white fish, salmon and prawns into the white sauce, place in ovenproof dish. Top with potatoes, mashed if old, sliced if new. Sprinkle the top with grated cheese and breadcrumbs. Place in hot oven for about half an hour.

SEAFOOD THERMIDOR

1/4 lb cooked white fish.

Fresh crab or quarter of a block of 50/50 frozen crabmeat.

Prawns.

1/4 pint white sauce flavoured with English mustard.

Chopped walnuts, breadcrumbs and grated cheese.

METHOD

Mix fish, crab and prawns together, fold into sauce. Place in ovenproof scallop shells. Pop into hot oven for 15 minutes. Sprinkle with mixed nuts, breadcrumbs and cheese. Place under a hot grill – watch as it burns very easily, as I know to my cost.

To check that these dishes have heated through, poke a round-bladed knife into the centre, remove and place on the back of your hand – quickly! If it feels hot so it will be in the centre of the dish.

CUSTOMERS — THE LIFE-BLOOD OF BUSINESS

WHY, I OFTEN ASK MYSELF, do customers always sit at the one uncleared table in the restaurant? Every table, bar one, can be cleared down, crumbs and spillage wiped up, napkins and sugar replenished, but which one do the customers sit at? The dirty one. Is this because they hope that they will be served quicker as someone will soon appear to clear it and will take their order? Well, this can backfire if there is a change of staff as the new staff may look around the dining room and assume that the dirty china belongs to the people sitting there. Of course in an ideal world, at the change-over, the new staff will be briefed as to what exactly is going on in the dining room, what stage in a meal a customer is at and who is sitting where. Unfortunately on hectic days this didn't always happen. I used to be annoyed at signs in other establishments asking one to wait to be seated, but in fact it is very wise. Even when Rob was in charge of the dining rooms people could sneak in and sit unobtrusively at a table while he was talking to a chatty soul.

When we took over Mary's many of the customers were very much of the old school and we had to watch our Ps and Qs, remembering not to get too familiar. On the odd occasion when we strayed over the line we were firmly put in our place. Having been told that Mr M was a regular, Rob went into the dining room to meet him for the first time. Sticking out his hand, he said "Good morning. My name is Rob, what do I call you?"

"I'm Mr M," came the answer in glacier tones, accompanied by an icy stare.

Many years later Mr M took Rob on one side and said in a conspiratorial tone: "I think, Rob, we have both served our apprenticeship. You may call me Jack." I'm not sure whether Rob touched his forelock or not.

Mrs W remained Mrs W until about two years before we retired when she suddenly asked us to supper. From then on we were allowed to call her Marjorie, but dear old Mrs K was Mrs K and we were Mr and Mrs Jelliff right up to the end – even though we suggested we might be less formal.

COME INTO THE GARDEN

Some of our customers had very strange ideas about the garden. If people wanted to eat in the garden we hoped they would give their orders at the back door or at the cake kitchen window. Of course there were occasions when customers would throw the system (Occasions? They were *always* doing it!) and wander into the dining room to place an order.

"Are you sitting outside?" we would ask politely.

"No, we are in the garden."

One lady came in highly incensed. "Do you know you've got *wild birds* in your garden?"

And then another. "I need to have the name of your insurance company. I've got a spot on my skirt from a bird dropping and I'm going to make a claim." Every morning when the weather was nice Rob went out with water and a sponge and washed down every table and stool. But there was a limit.

A lady came in with an empty plate. "I have a complaint to make."

"So sorry to hear that. What is the problem?"

"I was offering a blackbird a little piece of doughnut. It put its head on one side and looked me in the eye as if to say 'you have to be joking,' then it hopped along the table and took the rest of the doughnut off my plate."

With relief we laughed with the lady.

One year our neighbour decided that he would join in the 'Good Life' and bought some chickens – free range chickens. These fowl, not being stupid, soon found that once they had negotiated the garden fence, there were rich pickings to be had from gullible tourists handing out titbits. This was fine for a while, but in the second year, after many spring hatchlings and much cooing over the dear little balls of fluff, the aforementioned grew up and we were overrun by them. Customers' complaints came in thick and fast: scones were being snaffled, tables were a mess, in fact people were being terrorised by the chickens! Something had to be done. Rob manfully went next door and mildly asked if the chickens could be kept under control. Our neighbour wasn't exactly happy but made pointed remarks about townies not understanding rural life. After that the number of birds did decrease, but by what method I don't think we will go into. I promise that chicken didn't feature largely on the menu.

On his first August bank holiday in the Met, Colin was given leave and came home to stay, bringing with him his friend Mick, ex-Royal Marine. Obviously one year away from the business had blanked Colin's mind to the chaos that this holiday brought to Mary's, as he arrived around lunch-time expecting a fond welcome and a leisurely meal. The reality was very different. The world had fallen in on us; everyone was madly flying around and as soon as Colin appeared a pad was thrust into his hand.

"Take an order on table six," his harassed father said, rushing off before Colin could argue. Mick was also press-ganged into helping. He was asked to take trays out into the garden for the boys and girls, where he was to call names and deliver teas.

In retrospect this was probably not such a good idea. Mick is well over six foot, well-built and at this time his hair was very short, making a rather threatening figure, not one's idea of a friendly helpful waiter at a cosy seaside tea room, especially as he was sporting a T-shirt that pronounced *Captain Napalm. Death*! When customers did not respond at once to his first call, as was often the case, Mick would repeat it in a loud, somewhat belligerent, tone. A cowering customer would raise a hand somewhat nervously and the tray would be delivered. Probably without a smile.

Little Michael, so-called to distinguish him from washing-up Michael, always delivered his trays with a charming smile. One morning he came back from the garden somewhat deflated.

"What's wrong, Mike?" we asked.

"Well," he said. "This customer's name was Benz, so when I took him his coffee I asked if the Mercedes in the car park was his. He just shook his head and said 'No, we came on ze bicycles.' Well, I thought it was funny."

Rob got into trouble from the youngsters when a young man came to the back window where Rob was taking garden orders. The order was written down

"Name, please, sir," said Rob.

"Jones," came back the answer. Much muttering back-stage.

"Rob, didn't you recognise him? He's Griff Rhys Jones."

Many famous people patronised our little restaurant over the years.

The Freuds, of course. They live in the village a few doors away from the restaurant and Jill runs the very popular Summer Theatre in Southwold. One of our girls got into severe trouble from Sir Clement when he sat for ages over his tea and she needed to set up for dinner. She tried to surreptitiously polish the tables, but he chastised her for filling the air with the smell of polish while he was drinking his tea.

Cleo Lane and Johnny Dankworth were easy to spot as they drove in in their Rolls, CLEO 1. What an exceedingly charming couple they were.

Pam Ayres was very reserved when she was recognised and sat with her back to the dining room. Not the friendly person she seems on telly.

Then there was Jane Asher, who was kept waiting for ages for a table. Shortly after her visit she opened her own tea-room.

Helen McDermott of Anglia Television had half an idea about buying Mary's, but she came on a very busy Sunday afternoon and changed her mind.

The boys and girls recognised many faces from various soaps and were very impressed. I'm afraid we didn't score too well on knowing them. No time to watch soaps in this business.

NO-PAYERS

We found that on the whole customers were very honest. We only knowingly had four no-payers. The first incident was a lovely sunny day when a large family group came into the garden where they had the usual doughnuts, cakes and scones. Lizzie, one of our youngsters, had served them. Usually garden customers paid when they ordered, but for some reason this party hadn't any change or some such story. They promised to pay when they brought their tray back. Time went by and Lizzie became aware that they had neither paid nor returned their tray (a cardinal sin!), so she went into the garden to see if they were still there. No. Only two tables, covered in dirty crocks.

Back she came to the kitchen. Had anyone taken their money? No. So the chase began. She and Rob got on their bikes and scoured the village, finally catching up with the party at the bailey bridge

that crosses the Blyth River into Southwold.

The family looked rather sheepish when Rob tactfully mentioned that they had forgotten to pay. The man said he thought his mother had paid. The mother was absolutely devastated. Whether the man was well aware that the bill wasn't paid I don't know, but mother obviously wasn't.

We had no doubt in another instance. A family of four came in for sausage and chips. They had their meal, then mother and one child left, then a little while later

Mick was press-ganged into helping

father and the other child went. Staff consultation: had anyone taken their money? No! Again Rob was on the case. This time he espied father half-way down the road and caught up with him. "Sir," he said politely, "your bill has not been settled." At which the man shouted down the road to his wife, who was fast disappearing around a corner. "Ma, you forgot to pay the bill." Had she? I wonder, but she paid with forced grace.

Another man came in for a snack with his son and we never did catch him. What an example to the children!

Rob was on the back door when one of the members of the Summer Theatre asked him if she could have a cream tea, but she had left her purse behind and would pay later. "Of course," said Rob. A sucker for a pretty face, I said nastily when it transpired that she never did pay for the cream tea. From then on whenever Rob saw her on stage or screen he would say "She still owes me for a cream tea." I was always half-afraid he might stop a live performance and demand his £2.50.

A lady came to the back door asking for the proprietor. She had found a wallet on the lawn. Had anyone lost one? she asked Rob. "No," he replied, "but I can put it in our safe until someone claims it." The lady was rather wary and said no, she would take it to Southwold Police Station, as there was rather a lot of money in it. Should anyone claim it, she said, that is where it would be. We had been about to take Gem out so we continued on our way without telling the staff about the errant wallet.

On our return we found the place being turned upside down. A man had asked about his wallet and was in a bit of a state as there was £1,500 in it. When Rob said calmly there was nothing to worry about as it was at the Police Station, the staff turned on him: why hadn't he let them know? They had hunted everywhere and Patricia had even waded through the rubbish sacks. She had every right to be annoyed.

THE THINGS PEOPLE ASK

Some of the questions people asked about the food were amusing. Some definitely were not.

"Is your fish fresh?" was a good one.

"No, we leave it out overnight so it smells ripe in the morning."

Or: "Are your chips greasy?"

"But of course."

On taking a high tea order, Rob was asked: "Are your sausages nice?"

Without blinking an eyelid Rob replied: "Frankly, sir, they're bloody awful."

The man looked decidedly taken aback as well he might. Rob continued: "Well, sir, what did you expect me to say?"

The man agreed that his question was rather silly and ordered the offending sausages. When he had eaten them he declared them first rate.

When I tried Rob's trick with the description of the meal, it nearly went horribly wrong. Mr W, a rather fussy little man, stopped me in the hall. "Well, Felicity, have you anything nice on the menu today?"

Feeling frivolous — or perhaps bloody-minded, — I replied: "Mr W, everything is pretty awful today."

No polite smile at this unfortunate joke, but an incredulous stare. "Oh, then I had better just have a salad."

It took a lot of persuading that this was not a serious answer before Mr W would change his mind and have something hot off the main menu. He always viewed me with suspicion after that and we gave each other a wide berth.

People often ask what the chef recommends. I feel this can be dangerous – if the lamb dish isn't moving, that's what the chef would recommend, regardless of whether it is his favourite dish.

Rob's advice was often asked in relation to what wine he would suggest to go with the meal. Some people went as far as to tell him to choose the wine for them. A great compliment. On the other hand there were some clients who wanted to impress their guest and I think this is where true customer care comes in. A young man came in on what seemed to be a first date.

"We'll have Kir Royal!" he said with great aplomb. Now did he mean it? Did he expect us to open a bottle of champagne to make the cocktail and to charge accordingly? Tactfully he was asked, "That's the white wine and cassis cocktail is it sir?" To which he agreed. He felt good because he knew as much as the waiter and wasn't stung in the pocket. On the other hand should his error have been corrected so he wasn't ripped off elsewhere?

"I would like a sweet white wine to go with our roast beef," another customer said. Repressing a shudder, Rob recommended a wine.

"No," the customer said. "I think we would like number twenty. It says it's sweet on the list."

Yes it did, a sweet dessert Sauterne, the most expensive wine on the list and definitely not to be drunk with roast

"I think you might find that rather *too* sweet," Rob tried tactfully to dissuade him from this disastrous choice but the customer was adamant. This was the wine he wanted. Rob capitulated and brought the offending Sauterne for the customer to try. To give him his due, he smiled ruefully and agreed that it was very sweet and that Rob was right.

What could one do? Refuse point blank to sell the customer the wine – which I believe some establishments do. This wasn't our style. The customer is always right – even when he's wrong, Rob would always counter.

ALCOHOL LAWS

Our wine was supplied locally. We tried English vintage but very rarely did it sell. Every year we changed the list always including one or two of my favourite wines. I wonder why?

English Licensing Laws were quite incomprehensible to visiting foreigners, and even to us on some occasions. When we took over, the law said that no alcohol could be served in the afternoon. We even had to take the optics off the wall! Hot summer afternoons would come and so would people gasping for a beer which we had to refuse to sell them.

That was easier than when alcohol could be served all day. We had a restaurant licence which allowed us to serve alcohol only with a 'plated meal'. Nowhere is one told what a plated meal is. We even asked a JP who came up with an extremely vague explanation so we played it by ear, but a straight request for a beer had to be refused.

A group of what we unkindly called 'Loud London Money' was making a bit of a scene in the hall, so I went out to investigate. The man was giving one of my girls a hard time, demanding gins all round.

"Is there a problem?" I asked, possibly sweetly.

"No, we want a gin and this young lady won't give us one."

"Then I'm afraid there is a problem as the law says we can't serve alcohol without a meal."

"Cook us steaks all round then," came the arrogant reply. "And then put them in the bin."

"I have no steak," I said: "so I'm afraid you'll have to go elsewhere."

Similarly on a busy Sunday afternoon a couple were shown to a table and Rob went to take the order.

"A Southern Comfort," the man ordered.

"I beg your pardon?" Bad manners were not tolerated at Mary's.

"I said, a Southern Comfort."

Rob replied pleasantly: "And is it sir's intention to eat with us?"

"No, it isn't."

"I'm terribly sorry but I can't serve you alcohol if you don't."

The man got up in a threatening attitude. "I have to say I don't like your manner," he said. "You can think yourself lucky I don't thump you." He turned to his unfortunate partner. "Come on, girl — we're getting out of here."

Needless to say all the other customers watched this scene with great interest and although they didn't actually clap when the couple left, there was a good deal of "Well done, Rob. You can do without that sort."

ATTITUDES AND FOIBLES

If customers came in with a bit of an attitude there wasn't much one could do about it. Perhaps they'd had a row, had bad news or didn't want to come in the first place. One could but try and jolly them along. Sometimes it worked and sometimes it didn't, as Rob found out.

"The lady on table nine is really miserable," one girl was heard to say and remembering what Gerald Milsom said about being in the business of entertainment, Rob rose to the challenge and swanned into the dining room to have a word. Approaching the table he smiled at the blue-rinsed lady sitting there. "Is all well?"

"No it is not," was the tart reply. "I can never understand why you restaurateurs put such rich food on the menu. Why don't you have things like steamed fish or simply boiled potatoes? I can eat that type of food."

"Well," said Rob, never at a loss, "we do put plainer food on the menu at lunch time, but in the evening." He was getting into full flow about how in the evening the food and the ambience should be more exciting, to think of dinner as more of an entertainment rather than just a meal, when the lady cut him short.

"Oh, do go away, young man," she said, "my evening has been spoilt enough as it is."

Exit one deflated Robert.

Later, I was told that she finished her meal with one of our luscious chocolate nut sundaes – nothing plain about them!

Although lunch officially ended at two p.m., if people came in shortly afterwards we would stretch a point. That is unless *we* were particularly stretched instead. The staff having had their lunch, Rob and I would sit down for ours in the relative privacy of the small dining room.

One day as I walked from the kitchen a couple came in to be greeted by Mel and were seated. Before sitting down I went to have a word with the remaining couple finishing their lunch, an elderly mother and her daughter who came in quite often. As I was chatting to them I overheard the newly-arrived woman giving her husband a really hard time. Selfish, I heard. Inconsiderate, unreasonable and so on. Leaving the regulars I smiled at our new table on my way past, to be greeted by a steely glare. While we ate our lunch we heard Mel asking them what they would like.

"Are we too late for lunch?" the man tentatively asked.

"I'll just ask the kitchen." Mel disappeared and returned to say: "The cook will do any of the fish dishes." They ordered the inevitable fish and chips.

Our lunch finished, I thought perhaps I ought to go and see if all was well (unusually, as this was Rob's forte). Luckily it was. Then the wife treated me to a diatribe against her poor husband. *He* had 'selfishly' wanted to walk to Dunwich for lunch, although he knew that she hadn't got sensible shoes on. *She* had wanted to have lunch *here* but *he* had left it so late that they couldn't get to Dunwich in time for lunch *there* anyway. It had nearly been too late to have lunch *here*, and so on. I was so thankful, for the poor man's sake, that we had been able to give them a meal. Finally I got away and scuttled into the kitchen and didn't reappear until they had gone. Mrs R and her daughter were still there. I went over to them.

"Sorry about the floor show," I said.

"That's all right," replied the daughter. "But that wasn't all."

"Really?" What was coming now?

"The wife came over and asked what I was eating. I said it was a chocolate nut sundae. She said didn't I know that they were bad for me so I replied, I know that but I can't resist one of Felicity's puddings. The woman stared at me and said perhaps I ought to look in the mirror!"

I was speechless, but the daughter thought the remark was funny. Evidently the woman's parting shot, when she passed the dresser displaying our jams for sale, was that as they were so full of sugar they ought to be banned. Perhaps if she had eaten a little more sugar she wouldn't have been so sour!

People became very possessive about which table they sat at. Mr W came unannounced for lunch with two lady friends and demanded table three. Unfortunately it had already been requested by another customer and booked accordingly. Mr W was a bit grim throughout his lunch. When he left he said he had enjoyed his meal and would like to book again, but this time he must have table three. His order was duly written in the book and off he went. The week before he was due, he rang to check his booking and that he was to sit at table three – yes he was. He rang the day before, and again on the morning of the lunch. He even called in midmorning to make sure that we were giving him the correct table. Lunchtime came and so did he, sitting on the right table.

I don't think he ever came again: perhaps it was a lifetime's ambition realised!

Table three was the most popular. Certainly Grace and her husband liked it as well, but at a pinch would put up with four or four-and-a-half. They would never book. On one famous occasion Grace arrived and all three tables were occupied. To say that she was put out was an understatement. Frances came into the kitchen in a bit of a tizzy.

"Grace is telling me to ask people to leave her table so that she can sit there, but I can't do that, can I?"

No, we agreed, she couldn't. Out she went back into the dining room to coax Grace onto another table, but Grace wasn't having a bit of it. Back came Frances.

"She is now telling me to get Rob. She says that he will know what to do."

So Rob was duly found. With great tact and a good deal of friendly persuasion, he guided Grace and husband to another table where they sat glowering at our other unfortunate guests. When the people from table three finally got up to leave, Grace leaned over and said without any grace at all: "You know, you were sitting at *my* table!"

It was always very touching to see the faith our little old ladies had in Rob. He was a great success with them, and they thought that his culinary prowess knew no bounds. I would hover close to tables when Rob, the non-cook, was asked how things were made. It made interesting listening. I would smile when I overheard them say: "Ask Rob. He knows how I like my fish cooked," or even instruct me to ask him how things should be done.

I know this is disloyal to my dear husband, but really he hasn't a clue, although I will say that he can manage a very superior cheese on toast. One evening I was going out and he had to get his own supper. As he has a great liking for baked beans I thought this would be a 'nice easy meal'.

"Open the beans and place them as they are in the microwave, just cover them with cling film," I said rushing out, late as usual. On my return Rob said: "The microwave sparked a bit when I put the beans in." Yes, he had put the beans in 'as they were' – I assumed he would know to put them in a plastic container.

Which just goes to show, one should always be very clear with one's instructions, and never — *never* — assume.

COINCIDENCES

Now we come to what became known as the 'Australian Story' so often was it recounted. At the time both Pennie and Colin were working in London. Colin was a PC stationed at Paddington Green. Pennie was in desktop publishing and this weekend she decided to come home for a break from city life. On the Saturday morning a customer, who was booked in with a party that evening called in to ask if it was all right to settle his bill on his Australian bank account.

"Of course," said Rob, not really knowing if it was or not.

The evening came and went and the party seemed to go with a swing. The bill was duly settled with the Australian cheque.

Next morning we took Pennie to Darsham, our nearest train station for her return journey to London — and who was on the station but our Australian couple. Rob introduced them to Pennie. The train pulled in, Rob helped with the cases and we waved them all on their way. We returned to Walberswick to face another day of fun and pleasure.

At about 3.30, with the lunch session over, we were sitting over a coffee when the telephone rang. One of the girls called Rob telling him that Colin wanted to speak to him.

"Hello, father." Usually this formal way of address meant trouble.

"Hello, Colin."

"What's this I hear about you cashing a cheque on an Australian bank account?"

"How?" Rob was amazed. "What?" Quite incoherent, unusual for him.

Colin told the tale. Our Australians had duly arrived in London and gone to their hotel where they had been asked for their vouchers from their travel agent. Consternation. They were not to be found, nor were any other of the documents that they needed. The hotel staff pointed them in the direction of the nearest police station to report their loss. The station was Paddington Green. The desk sergeant was Colin.

The man had gone to the desk. "Can you help me, officer?" The man explained about the loss.

"I'll have to take some details. Where were you staying before this?"

"Oh, in Suffolk"

"Where in Suffolk?"

"A little place called Walberswick. I'll spell that for you"

"I think I can spell that, thank you, sir," said Colin. He went on to ask: "And did you do anything interesting during your visit?"

"We went to Southwold and we went out to dinner last night at a place called Mary's."

"Oh, yes," said Colin. "Was it a good meal?"

"Excellent."

At this point Colin showed the man his warrant card. "Does this name look familiar to you? Mary's is owned by my parents."

The couple wouldn't believe him, so Colin had rung us up to prove the point. Rob, when telling the tale would always say, "So within twenty-four hours they had met all the Jelliff family" and we would say "Wow"!

One gorgeous summer evening we were sitting in the garden before opening for dinner when a fine vintage open-top car drove into the car park. A couple got out and strolled over to us.

"Isn't it a lovely evening?" they said. We all agreed.

"Do you have a table for dinner?" Yes, we had.

"Well we don't know whether to stay or not." We were non-committal.

"We thought it might be romantic to drive to Aldeburgh in the sunset and have fish and chips."

"Yes," we said, "it would be."

"On the other hand the sun might set before we get there. Do you think it will?"

We agreed that it might well set if they didn't go at once.

"Yes, we will. But we might be back." They gave a gay little laugh and a cheery wave before setting off.

Half an hour later they were back – the sun had set! Nastily, we had hoped that by the time they returned, we would be full. Unfortunately we weren't.

THOSE SPECIAL OCCASIONS

We catered for all sorts of occasions: birthday parties, firm's Christmas bashes, wedding receptions and funeral wakes. The latter could be sad, especially when it was someone we knew.

We had a special birthday booked; they wanted to come early, which was absolutely fine. The car park was empty when in drove the guests in two Rolls-Royces. The first one parked sedately, the second equally ponderously reversed — straight into it. Birthday boy had been driving and he stayed in the damaged car and sulked. He had to be cajoled out to come in and have dinner. Meanwhile the rest of the party came in and had drinks in the Snug. One of the ladies picked up a basket we were selling in our craft corner.

"What do you think?" she said coquettishly, walking up and

down with it on her arm.

"Lovely, dear," said her sister. "All you need is the pegs."

Another such was an eightieth birthday. Ian came down to book for the party and to prime Rob about his father-in-law.

"Sir M does like a bit of fuss," he said.

"Fine," said Rob. "I can touch the forelock and bend the knee."

"He also likes a large sherry – medium dry," Ian added.

The day arrived and the birthday party came and drinks were dispensed.

"Sherry, Sir M?" said Rob offering him a schooner.

"Thank you, my boy." The sherry was taken, consumed, and another was produced, which was quickly drunk.

Lunch came and went. All seemed to be well.

The next day Ian called in to settle the bill.

"Sir M enjoyed his lunch," said Ian. "Just one complaint."

"Oh dear," said Rob. "What was wrong?"

"He thought your measures of sherry were particularly parsimonious. But then," he added, "he would. At home, he drinks his sherry from a tumbler."

FOLLOW-ON

On one of not quite so far-flung holidays, this time to Jordan, we met a delightful couple, Alan and Angela. We were part of a small group touring this friendly little Arab country which is so different from England, and if you're wondering how this ties in with Walberswick, please be patient. Our first mini-adventure: on arrival at Amman Airport there was a power cut and we wandered about in semi-darkness trying to find our tour guide who, after the initial greeting, had disappeared.

Another *fracas* was when Rob and Alan had been for a float in the Dead Sea (you *can't* swim) and narrowly missed being arrested by the religious police. After coming ashore they found there was a queue for the shower block. Now both of them had been to boarding school where modesty was not an issue, so they ignored the greasy high-density water on their bodies and started to change in the communal area, much to the consternation of the Arabs. An English-speaking student quietly took them on one side and told them that it was against the law to show certain bits of themselves in public.

Later, Alan was on a pilgrimage to Petra and hoped to find the cave where he had slept rough during a campaign in the Second World War. On this trip we had the experience of riding ponies along the *wadi* into Petra city through the crack in the cliffs, to be confronted by the beautiful sight of brilliant sunlight shining on the amazing Treasury building. It was a magic moment. Another day Rob and I walked into Petra in the dark and up to the High Place of Sacrifice to see the sunrise, but the sky was covered in cloud, no sun. Not magic. I believe another way has been opened up into Petra and now cars and coaches can drive in. A terrible shame: the peace and quiet must be quite shattered.

Now here's the local link: the fact that we were restaurateurs came into discussion and Angela and Alan said they would come and see us in Walberswick. People were always saying this, but promises — or threats — never materialised. However, Alan and Angela's did. I had discovered that treacle sponge was one of Alan's favourite puddings, so on the night they came I decided to put it on the dinner menu. This was not a pudding I would normally have chosen as I tended to put light and fluffy creations on in the evening. To my surprise nearly everyone chose to have the sponge, so I had to make sure I put some aside for Alan. It was a reminder of happy times in Jordan.

The reverse sometimes happened; customers would ask *us* to meet *them* socially. "If we invited you, would you come to dinner?" We had been advised not to mix business with pleasure, probably sound advice, but we didn't comply and frequently accepted invitations, sometimes with surprising results.

An elderly couple came quite regularly. She was always smartly dressed, and he wore tweeds, a rather taciturn individual. We had put him down as a retired Suffolk farmer. When asked, we said we would be delighted to go to dinner. On the requisite evening we donned our glad rags and drove to our destination. We knocked on the door which was opened by John, tieless, sporting a cardigan, braces and carpet slippers. To say we felt overdressed was an understatement. John showed us into the sitting room and asked us what we would like to drink. Not sure what might be available I muttered something about a dry sherry.

"Nina," shouted John to his wife, who was in the kitchen. "Have we any of that sherry that was left over from Christmas?"

It was now round about March. Rob and I exchanged looks, wondering what had we got ourselves into and were we even expected? We felt decidedly snobbish. I hurriedly said that if it was a problem a martini would be fine, but a sherry was found and a quite acceptable one too.

Nina came through and said that dinner was ready and would we like to come to the table. She hoped we liked grouse. Suddenly we were reversing our earlier preconceptions as we found we had stepped into something well-planned.

The table was beautifully laid with linen, silver and crystal and at each place setting was a plate of seafood delightfully garnished. As we sat down, John said: "I think you'll like this wine. You carry a Pulham vineyard wine. This is from the same grower but this is his special *cuvée*. You can't buy it as they make only a few bottles, but I happen to know the owner very well."

Indeed it was delicious. While Nina cleared for main, John poured a red wine from a cut glass decanter. Rob gently swirled the dark ruby in his glass.

"Well, John, I don't know what this is but I think you've spoilt us."

He certainly had. The wine was a 1964 La Tâche. Although, to be absolutely honest, I didn't like it as much as Rob did, who went into raptures over it. (A friend of ours always says: "Don't tell *me* how good a wine is if I don't like it.")

The grouse was wonderful. With pudding, John produced a *Trockenbeerenauslese*. And then standards changed again and we watched bemused as he poured some into a saucer and called his dog.

"I don't like this sweet stuff, but the dog does."

With coffee we were offered liqueurs or brandy which I declined — someone had to drive home. Rob was given a 1923 vintage Armagnac. After this John said to Rob: "Would you like to see my wine cellar?" Of course Rob would. He needed no second bidding. Off went the men while I helped Nina with the washing up! Bless her — as soon as the men disappeared she lit up a cigarette.

"John doesn't like me to smoke," she said. "I hope you don't mind?"

On the way home Rob told me that John had a double garage out the back piled high with cases of wine – you name it, he had it. When Rob queried storing wine in a garage, John told him that as long as the temperature change was slow it didn't matter too much what it was, unless of course it was too extreme. (When one of our travels took us to Namibia we had to return three bottles of wine that had oxidised. When we asked how the wine was stored we were told at room temperature — African room temperature, over ninety degrees Fahrenheit.)

John was no farmer; he was a wine merchant, which just goes to show one should never judge people by their appearances, as my children are always telling me.

Sadly, shortly after this gastronomic experience we heard that Nina had died and that John had moved away.

Over the years regular customers got to know each other quite well. In fact the Luncheon Club seemed to be just that, a select club with customers stopping to chat with other members, a lovely atmosphere. On occasions I still hear some of our friends say to each other, "How did you meet Felicity and Rob?"

"At Mary's."

"Oh yes."

I do a little outside catering for some of our previous customers and learn that some of them have kept up with old friends. Perhaps I should arrange an 'Old Mary's Reunion'?

On the other hand it has been known for some customers to ask if they might leave through the kitchen rather than meet someone coming through the front door. Or ask to be seated in a different dining room!

Our customers varied from babes in arms to elderly guests in wheelchairs.

The older people always dressed for dinner and made an occasion of it but increasingly we noticed that the young were happy to wear jeans and a t-shirt. Perhaps with more affluence, eating out was no longer an occasion, especially in a humble little establishment like ours in a tiny village like Walberswick. Patricia and I would tut-tut in the kitchen deploring the fall in standards.

But when a young man came in for tea with no shirt on at all, I did have to go out and 'have a word.'

"I wonder," I said, possibly not sweetly, "if you would mind putting on your shirt."

"Don't you like my body?" came the aggressive reply.

"Not particularly," I said.

Somewhat deflated he put on the shirt. Stuffy, no doubt some would say, but I wouldn't want to have my afternoon tea looking at a sweaty, hairy torso!

Rob had a similar run-in with a young lady. Not because she was topless, I hasten to add, but because her t-shirt was covered with obscene words. Her boyfriend said to her, "I told you not to wear that shirt out to tea." She was quite repentant and sat with her back to the wall and her arms crossed over her front. Quite difficult to eat and drink like that I should think. Trouble is, I never did find out what the t-shirt said.

DRAMBUIE STEAK

One small onion diced finely.
Butter and a little olive oil.
8 oz fillet steak cut in strips.
Small carton double cream.
Drambuie to taste.
Seasoning.

METHOD

Melt butter and olive oil on moderate heat, add diced onion –
cook until softened. Raise the heat, when pan is hot quickly add the
steak. Toss meat while it cooks, add Drambuie. When hot add the
cream and seasoning. Stir until the sauce is thick, smooth and
lightly brown, serve at once.

STEAK AND KIDNEY PUDDING

1/2 lb self-raising flour.
A little baking powder. Seasoning.
4 oz suet.
A little water.
One small diced onion.
1 lb stewing steak cut into cubes.
Cubed kidney – *I only get a little as I'm not too keen on it but it does add
to the flavour.*
Seasoned flour.

METHOD

Make the suet pastry: sieve flour, seasoning and baking powder
together. Mix in the suet, add a little water and mix to a soft dough.
Roll out pastry. Line a pudding basin – leave enough pastry for a
lid. Toss onion and meats in seasoned flour, place in pudding basin.
Add a little more water, top with the pastry lid. Cover the top with
greaseproof paper and foil or use pudding basin with its own lid.
Place in a saucepan third-filled with hot water and cook for five
hours. Do not allow to boil dry.

PUBLICITY

I don't think it is too much of an exaggeration to say that Mary's was known world wide. We had customers from all over the globe and regulars who had holidays abroad would tell us of occasions when they had seen our card stuck up in many strange places. As might be expected I wasn't always named as the best ambassador.

Once a year a group of Dutch boys sailed over from Holland and always came for meals. After thirteen years we got to know them quite well. They forgave us when on their first visit they heard a rendition of the old Amsterdam song 'I saw a mouse – where?' coming from the kitchen. Likewise when they asked us if this bit of the sea had any special name.

"It's Sole Bay," I said. "Remember we had a sea battle there against the Dutch, which we won," I added with glee.

"What about the Medway?" they countered, quoting an encounter the English had lost.

"Ah," I said. "We don't talk about that."

When the recession hit east Suffolk and trade fell off, we had to rack our brains for ideas on how to drum up trade, especially on Friday evenings. Colin and Corrina, who were still living with us, suggested that we might try theme evenings, one a month. We were rather cautious about this because at the time nothing like it had been tried in the area.

"All the more reason for us to give it a go," the young ones said.

Also I wasn't altogether sure I knew enough about different cuisines to put together a menu. Finally we said that if they organised the evening, we would back them. The first one was Greek; it was a tremendous success. We could have booked the tables twice over. This gave us confidence and we went on to other things: Jewish, Russian, Swedish and so on. We did lots of research and went shopping in obscure places for authentic ingredients, wines and liqueurs. Possibly we didn't make much money but the restaurant was full and it was great fun.

Even so we received several phone calls.

"I'd like to book a table for Friday night."

"What time would you like to come?"

"Seven-thirty — but it isn't one of your special evenings, is it?"

One was tempted to say every evening at Mary's was special; instead one reassured them in a soothing tone it was in fact a normal evening. But what's 'normal'?

As things do, the novelty wore off, other restaurants were offering similar evenings and trade fell away, so we returned to the usual menu and the drawing board.

Our final promotional idea was the Friday Luncheon Club. Members paid a fee to join, the momentous sum of £5, and we issued them with a card. We provided a restricted menu — three or four starters, three main, three puddings — at a reduced fixed price. This was received well and most members stayed with us until the end.

FESTIVE MEALS

We spent our first Christmas at home, but because of popular demand we did Christmas lunch every year thereafter, cajoling friends and family to help, even customers. For several years a family stayed in the flat above and we roped them in to get up early and put the oven on for the turkey, while we brought a second turkey from home in the back of the car. I had an automatic timer on my domestic cooker so didn't have to get up at the crack of dawn. The menu never varied but that was what people wanted.

When people were assembling in the Snug we handed them a drink and offered cheese aigrettes, then at the appropriate hour we showed them to their seats and they sat down to smoked salmon tastefully garnished, followed by Champagne sorbet. I had made this well in advance, then the day before, we scooped it into the requisite number of flutes, so it could be quickly taken to the table – the alcoholic content being high it would melt very quickly.

While we cleared and got organized, Rob and a hijacked helper would go round pouring respectable *petit chateau* claret or a little white number. Then out would go the turkey and all the trimmings. There was always a vegetarian option as there was always a vegetarian, some we knew and some we didn't.

"Oh, didn't I say Aunt Ethel was a vegetarian?"

Or the lady who said: "But I thought *everyone* knew I'm a vegetarian."

To follow we served peach and apple soufflé or Christmas pudding with brandy butter and cream. Not a drop of custard in sight!

We offered Asti to drink with this and finally walnuts and

Madeira. Rob would ask everyone to be upstanding and he would propose the loyal toast. Then a customer would toast the chef and all her helpers. The chef would mutter her thanks into her beard and retire in confusion into the kitchen to oversee the making of coffee. All very civilised!

We enjoyed the occasion. It was no sacrifice to work on the special day. After everyone had gone and all the washing-up and clearing had been done, we sat down and had our lunch. Even after it had stood around and then been microwaved it was a good meal, 'although I do say so myself, as one that shouldn't'. Family and friends came back with us to our house in Wenhaston where we spruced up, made smoked salmon sandwiches, then sat down, kicking off our shoes, drinking champagne and opening our presents.

Boxing Day was the day we celebrated. Even if it fell on a Sunday we didn't open. Rob would try and persuade us but Patricia and I always rebelled. A long walk was the order of the day before returning to cook dinner, Robert Carrier's Pheasant *à la crème*. It has always been our Christmas dish, a real treat. Rob would lay the table with all the best silver and crystal and we would dress for dinner. This little ritual made the meal rather special.

Our customers always wore their best for Christmas lunch which was rather nice. Only on our last commercial lunch did two teenagers come in jeans. Made me tut-tut in the kitchen and friend June and I looked at each other and complained about the lack of standards in the young!

One Christmas Patricia was the only professional member of the team, the rest being family and friends, so at the end of the session we handed her all the tips which she refused to accept, giving us all a fair share. This we gleefully spent in the pub on Boxing Day, which just happened to be on the route of our walk.

We didn't open for the last Christmas we were in harness as Patricia was away, as also were Colin, and Rob's brother and sister-in-law; and Pennie and Paul were spending the holiday with Paul's parents. That just left Rob and me. As we didn't think that we could do a very good job on our own we stayed firmly closed and went away ourselves.

One gentleman came only for Christmas lunch, but he complained vociferously. Where was he going to go? I don't think we were terribly sympathetic.

New Year's Eve wasn't a holiday we catered for after some customers sat snoozing gently in the bar until three a.m. the next year. I said that I wasn't prepared to work, so unless the holiday fell on a Friday or Saturday we saw the New Year in at home.

New Year's Day was a different matter altogether. This was the day we did the Victorian Breakfast which people would book from one year to the next. At about eleven a.m. guests would start to arrive. We greeted them with a glass of mulled wine then they would don outdoor gear and Rob would take them for a walk over the marsh or common for an hour or two. On their return they divested themselves and were given a glass of Bucks Fizz while they found their table. The menu was a straight crib from John Tovey, former owner-chef of Miller Howe on the shore of Windermere, and people loved it. How they managed to eat it all was a mystery to me.

After Buck's Fizz came grapefruit with chilled crème de menthe. That was a nightmare, cutting twenty to thirty grapefruits with a serrated edge. Pennie was brilliant at this, but she was only with us for about two of the breakfasts.

Porridge warmed people up. Rob went round with a bottle of Glenmorangie and a tablespoon. Try it for yourself: porridge with cream, brown sugar and a little malt — delicious, if you don't put on too much whisky and don't use a malt that tastes of burnt rubber. I think it was an Islay malt that Rob put on one year — I thought it was quite disgusting. We filled a puff pastry case with smoked haddock in a cheese sauce garnished with tomato and watercress. Just the one; there were several more courses to follow.

Devilled kidneys were the least popular dish, but most people tried it, especially as they were given a glass of burgundy to go with it.

Then we gave them a rest before the platter. Egg, bacon, mushroom, fried bread, tomato, sauté potatoes, chipolata and a slice of apple. I am afraid customers weren't given the option with their eggs of easy-over, sunnyside up and so on, although two customers always had their eggs cooked to destruction and all this washed down with a glass or two of claret.

If they had any room the meal was completed with toast, jam, tea or coffee. After which, people waddled home.

During each course we gave the staff a sample. Needless to say we never had any problems staffing this day even if some of our young men looked a bit green around the gills! When all our guests had gone we tidied up, sat down and had our platter. Except for one bright and sunny New Year when we foolishly served a small party with tea. Suddenly the dining-rooms were full of customers who had ignored our *closed* signs and were demanding all sorts of culinary delights, even fish and chips! We were not happy bunnies.

Occasionally we would do wine tastings. Our one-time dentist had retired and started up a little wine business called 'In the Pink'. From time to time we got together and arranged a meal to complement the wines. These were great as there was no choice on the menu (except for vegetarians) and one knew exactly how many people were coming. Usually I had a round of applause after the meal which appealed to my ego!

ADVERTISING — THE NAME GAME

How else to get more business? Advertising was possibly the answer, but paid-for it was expensive and didn't always pay off. Free advertising was what we needed. Our local paper ran a feature on local chefs so I put myself forward for that and to my surprise I was taken up. The interview took place and the photographs taken, quite good ones, too. What was my signature dish? What *was* my signature dish?

I had no idea; fish and chips hardly seemed to fit the bill, then I thought of *Bœuf à la nage*, a dish I had done for an 'In the Pink' wine tasting that would have to do. For one photograph I had to be seen making the dish and for another seated looking at it with satisfaction, which is what I hope it signified, not a self-conscious smirk!

The article was duly published. Unfortunately the paper forgot to mention where I worked. They rectified this in a later edition but placed the admission of omission in some obscure corner so we felt the value of the publicity was somewhat lost.

I had mentioned during the interview that we served steak and kidney pudding every Friday. Some alert gentleman had seen this, and the apology, and had come all the way from Bury St Edmunds to try it. He said that it was worth every minute of the journey, so *something* was salvaged from the article.

We always advertised in the programme for Jill Freud's Summer Theatre and several of the cast patronised our restaurant. One year we received a strange request from the assistant stage manager: could we save them the skeleton of a fish – preferably a herring? We told them it would have to be a sole but doubted if anyone could tell the difference. The skeleton was saved and delivered, and we got a mention in the programme — for supply of properties!

The next venture was an interview with Radio Norfolk. My sister-in-law Gill had heard us mentioned on some programme about local tearooms, so I thought I would ring them up and tell them I was the owner of one. Would they like an interview? Yes they would. Could I come in the next morning to be interviewed – live? Off I went, Rob driving me in as I was absolutely terrified and suffering from a rotten cold. I kept saying: "Next time I have a bright idea like this just remind me how scared I was."

However, the radio interviewers put me totally at my ease, I didn't 'dry' which was my greatest fear, and I loved every minute of it. So much so that for weeks afterwards I tried to think of excuses why I shouldn't go back. Rob sat in the car listening to the broadcast and said it was fine. Back at the ranch the staff had been listening and had taped it for me. 'Flick's first radio appearance,' Michael had written on the sleeve. First and only, but it brought in new people and old acquaintances.

"Heard you on the radio and thought we'd come and see you again."

I even did talks at the local WIs although how much good they were in drumming up trade is debatable as a friend told me that someone had told her that she had enjoyed a talk given by the lady who ran Mollies at Blythburgh. And that's the next village along!

After one WI talk a member started her vote of thanks by saying: "We all thought this talk was going to be boring, but in fact it has been very amusing."

Of course, being in the food guides helps a lot and over the years we were recommended in quite a few. We were in the Good Food Guide for a while but were dropped around the time *nouvelle cuisine* was all the vogue and it became rather pretentious. We rang to ask why we had been dropped but the answer was somewhat vague: someone had disagreed with something that had been written the year before. We also discovered that some guides expected to be paid a large fee before one was included. As they were horribly expensive we declined their offers.

Back on mundane business, one day at the end of lunch a gentleman came in and ordered a sandwich of which he ate a quarter, then he ordered a lemon cake and ate about two mouthfuls. Mel was concerned and so was I when he asked to see the proprietor. Frantically I looked around for Rob who had conveniently disappeared. In fear and trepidation I went out to see our fussy eater. Tentatively I asked: "Was everything all right?"

He smiled. "Is there somewhere we can talk in private?"

Feeling very uneasy at this point I nervously ushered him into the small dining room and shut the door.

He turned to me: "I expect you're wondering why I left all my lunch?"

"Well, yes," I said.

"I'm an inspector for a food guide, and you were the fourth establishment that I've visited this lunch time and to be honest I couldn't face another meal, however light. But I've seen enough to ask if you would like to be included in the book and would answer a few questions?" In my relief I was probably over-effusive in my replies.

One of the guides we featured in was *And Baby Came Too*. A mixed blessing. Well-behaved children were a joy but some could be absolute horrors, lying about on the floors. We knew whose fault it would be if hot water got inadvertently split on a child rolling on the floor. No 'please' and 'thank you' – just 'I want this – I want that'. We got some very funny looks from parents when we insisted on the magic word *please*.

Frequently we were asked if we served food suitable for children. This seemed strange to me as I thought children ate a smaller amount of whatever their parents ate. In the end we bowed to pressure and put fish fingers and similar items on a special menu for the little darlings, but we did draw the line at beef burgers. I invented some ice cream puddings to put on the children's menu, a chocolate banana boat and a baby bloomer (a small knickerbocker glory). I have to say more grown-ups than children asked for them! We got into terrible trouble with one mother as we gave her little precious a piece of fish with a bone in it – unknowingly, I hasten to add.

"I shall never come here again," she said. I think this must have been just before we retired, as Rob replied that he was very pleased to hear it.

Was it our fault to send out a piece of cod with a bone in it or was it the mother's responsibility to make sure it was bone free before the child ate it? Better still, a fillet of plaice could have been ordered with less possibility of a bone.

We received another lambasting from a mother because the egg we sent out for her child was lightly fried.

"Don't you follow government guidelines?" she shouted and insisted we fried another egg, then complained that the chips were cold. All at five past five when we closed at five p.m. And it had been a busy Sunday afternoon.

COACH PARTIES WELCOME

These were great fun. We had two standard menus for them: afternoon tea or high tea. The former consisted of three assorted sandwiches; one scone, jam and cream; a choice of cream cake; tea or coffee. For the latter they could choose fish, salad and chips, or a cold meat, salad and chips – the unfortunate vegetarians were offered a cheese salad. The numbers varied from twenty to fifty but forty was about par for the course. All being well, the sandwiches were made in the morning, covered with cling film and placed in the fridge. In the afternoon while the girls laid up, having chivvied late luncheon diners on their way or sat them in the Snug, the cooks would set out the sandwiches on individual plates, garnished with cucumber and tomato. Then the scones were buttered and a cake tray made up, creamed and decorated. Meringues were the favourite. The plan was for this to be done before the cry went up: "The coach is here!" This was the signal for the blackboard to go out saying: 'Today we welcome the Red Cross' or such like, and for the teapots and hot-water jugs to be filled and put on the tables. Rob would rush out and welcome the arrivals, trying to maintain some sort of order, but chaos usually reigned for a while.

"Where's Gladys?"

"I usually sit next to Maude."

"My husband is to sit here. I'm saving his place."

Then we would find a table laid for four had six people around it, complaining that there weren't enough sandwiches and cups and saucers, so we would try to steer some of them to a table laid for six where only two people were sitting. Finally Gladys would be found, Maude would be with her friend, and the husband restored to his wife, then peace would resume and the consumption of vast quantities of tea and cream cakes would take place.

Fish teas were a bit more stressful. When the booking was made, we were told how many wanted fish and how many for meat salad. That way the salads and side salads could be made up in advance. (One dreadful day the side salads were put in the fridge and forgotten, only to be discovered after we waved the coach goodbye). On the day there were always more people wanting fish than had actually ordered it. Probably Fred saw the fish and chips go out and thought that he would prefer them to a cold meat salad. On the other hand they had probably forgotten what they had ordered. I know I would have done! Some parties were very well organised and had a list of who had ordered what.

"No, Martha, you said fish and chips. It's on the list so that's what you're having."

After this they had an ice cream pudding, variety chosen on the day. Banana split was the great favourite. Sometimes we were known to run out of bananas and have to rush round to the Tuck Shop for fresh supplies.

The coach trippers always seemed to enjoy their afternoon, and so did we. Some parties came year after year, but it was sad to see some of the travellers become very frail. The Red Cross outing was a lesson to us all. With all their afflictions they were all extremely cheerful and joked with us throughout the afternoon. At the end of our time at Mary's the helpers had become as old as their charges. Although we did one last tea for them after we retired, at the village hall, the helpers said that they could no longer cope so the tea parties came to an end. So sad as they were enjoyed so much, and there were no younger people about willing to help.

A small church group who came annually always asked for the little dining room. After we had served tea they closed the doors. I didn't know what went on but it was awfully quiet.

MEALS ON FEET

One day we received a phone call.

"My name is Mrs J," said a quivery voice. "You don't know me but my son has just died and I have no one to look after me, so I wonder if you could help me?"

The outcome of this call was that every day when we were open we plated up a meal and took it down to Mrs J. When we were closed we produced dishes that could be frozen and we placed them in her freezer. She would ring in the morning and choose from the menu. This was fine when she rang early, but occasionally it would be gone twelve and we would be very busy, then it was impossible to send someone down with her lunch. We would dread the call that we knew would come, and a weeping voice saying:" Have you forgotten me?"

"No," we would say. "Just terribly busy. We'll be with you as soon as possible."

Occasionally Rob would take her meal down. On one visit he reported that she had a gun beside her chair and he didn't think that was a terribly good idea. On one of Colin's visits home we told him about this problem. At the time he was leading the firearms inquiry team. We thought Mrs J might listen to him, so we sent him down to have a word.

"Ah," said Mrs J. "This is only a replica so I can't shoot anyone." He explained that a burglar wouldn't know that and might hit her and ask questions later. We thought that she had seen the sense in this as the gun was no longer in evidence, but of course it could have been hidden under a cushion. Her son had been a gun dealer, so I don't know what else she had about the place.

Bless her, she loved to chat, being a lonely soul, but we didn't have much time when we were delivering her lunch. She told us that no one went to see her which was, as we found out, not true. When she said that she had lost her cleaner Roger volunteered for the job. I don't think a lot of cleaning was done but what she wanted was a cheerful person to chat to and Roger certainly filled the bill. She would explain that her feet hurt so much that she could hardly walk. We were of course very sympathetic. When she fell ill and was taken into hospital, it transpired that her toenails hadn't been cut since her son's death several years before. Poor old soul — the nails had grown into her feet. No wonder they were so painful.

We had two other ladies for whom we regularly did meals on foot. Lucy was a dear. Soup is what she loved and would always say: "Felicity, your soups are wonderful."

Not wanting to take credit where it wasn't due I would tell her that Patricia had made the soup but it was me she would always thank profusely.

Then there was Mrs G. I think that in a former life she must have lived abroad and had staff as she behaved accordingly. Frequently when we went down with her meal she would have disappeared. We would wander round shouting her name but to no avail so we would have to leave it on the doorstep. It was never there when we went the next day so either she found it or a passing dog had a good meal. Not a very satisfactory arrangement.

BREAD AND BUTTER PUDDING

White sliced bread 6-8 slices; butter for spreading.

4 oz sultanas. Sugar.

Two eggs and two egg yolks.

$\frac{1}{2}$ pint milk.

$\frac{1}{4}$ pint double cream.

Demerara sugar. Nutmeg.

METHOD

Butter an ovenproof dish. Set oven to 160 degrees. Butter the bread. Cut off crusts (these can be made into breadcrumbs). Place most of bread and butter on base of dish. Cover with sultanas and some sugar. Place remaining bread and butter on top of sultanas. Whip up eggs and milk and cream and a little sugar. Pour over bread and butter. Leave to soak for half an hour. Sprinkle sugar and nutmeg over the top.

One rather superior cooking writer said this dish was not the thing at all, but my customers liked it!

APPLE CHARLOTTE

1½ lbs cooking apples, peeled and sliced.
Demerara sugar.
White bread, at least 6-8 slices.
½ lb melted butter (wicked!).
Golden syrup.
A little extra butter.

METHOD

Slightly sweeten the apples. Place in plastic bowl, cover with cling film, make two holes, cook in microwave until a purée. Do be careful taking off the cling film. Butter the dish. Cut crusts off bread and cut into three. Dunk bread into melted butter and line the sides of the dish. Place apple purée into dish. Cover with dunked bread. Sprinkle the top with demerara sugar. Warm the syrup and drizzle some over the sugar, dot with butter. Cook in oven at 200 °C until the top is brown and crispy.

ACCIDENTS AND CATASTROPHES
MECHANICAL PROBLEMS

In the kitchen there were several bits of kit without which life was extremely difficult. Why was it they always went down on a busy Sunday or a Bank Holiday?

There was the cream machine. A wonderful invention. We would pour fresh cream into the top and when we pressed a button, the motor would whip up the cream to produce a piped offering onto the proffered receptacle. So precious was this machine only a chosen few were allowed to clean it. Once or twice the motor went down and we had to resort to the Kitchen Aid. This took a lot more time and time is of the essence when one is coping with a hundred cream teas. It also used a lot more cream, so *panic*! Would we have enough to last the session and was more ordered for the next day? I wonder if the day the Tuck Shop forgot to order our cream could be classed as a catastrophe? It certainly felt like it at the time – no doubt it was a bank holiday.

With its two-minute cycle it goes without saying the dishwasher was a godsend; even so on busy days we needed two washer-uppers. The machine was on its last legs when we inherited it but somehow we managed to keep it going. Of course when it had a funny turn it was always when we were at our most busy. Then there would be frantic telephone calls to washer-uppers past and present, not to mention friends who lived locally. Could they come and help? As a last resort Rob would get to the sink with much muttering and crashing but the washing-up got done in record time. He would wave at customers who might put their heads round the door to see where he was.

"And you thought I did nowt!" he would call out.

The Still provided us with non-stop boiling water. After a year we replaced the small one that was *in situ* as it just couldn't keep up with demand. When the hot water ran out an urn was put into play. This was highly dangerous in a busy kitchen. I would have nightmares about people scalding themselves, especially the youngsters, even though the 'babies' weren't allowed to use the still let alone the urn. It was a real pain to have to keep the urn topped up and to be around to fill up teapots and water jugs. However, even the new still would pack up and out would come the urn again and we would rush about begging and borrowing kettles from our neighbours.

One bank holiday — the memory of which is burned into my mind — the water supply was cut. After frantic phone calls it was ascertained that a water main had been fractured in Bramfield, seven miles away, and although it was being worked on, there would be no water until the morrow. There was some water in the still but not much, some in the dishwasher and our water tanks. Explanations were given to the queues at the back door as to why the water might have run out before we got to their order and what would they like instead of tea. Most of the customers were understanding. Some not.

"Squeeze the tap," one lady said. "I must have my cup of tea.."

At the end of trading we had to go next door with buckets and drain their water supply. This way we were able to clear and wash up.

The greatest catastrophe was of course the hurricane in October 1987. I remember that I had to drive to the dentist the day before. Even then the trees were bending about in an alarming manner, but I got home unscathed, even though trees were blown down behind me shutting off the road. At the time we were extending our sitting room, which was quite uninhabitable with one window out and one wall out, the ceiling supported by an RSJ. In the morning Rob reported a sleepless night. He felt as though the floor of our bedroom (which was situated above the sitting room) was being lifted up and might at any moment collapse. I slept through it all, unconscious that I was experiencing a rare phenomenon. Rob said later that he thought that if the wall hadn't been out we might have suffered some damage, but as it was the wind blew straight through!

I had to drive to Halesworth the next morning and the view of the Blyth valley was quite surreal with all the trees up-ended. "It must have been quite a blow," I said innocently, not having at that time heard the news and realising the extent of the damage nationwide. This was soon brought home to us with no electricity in Wenhaston and none in Walberswick. The road to and from work was clear so we could get to Mary's, but what to do when we got there?

Rob rustled up two camping gas stoves and we managed to keep going for a few days, even coping with dinner one evening. Candles everywhere — I don't know what the fire officer would have said about that. On those few days we saw people from the village who had never been in before and they never came again! It was of course a very limited menu getting less and less as the days went by. Soup and omelettes seemed to feature predominantly I seem to remember. Then as things started to defrost and with no fridges functioning, we had to concede defeat. I think we were without power for about a week in Walberswick but less at home. Our first job when things got back to normal was to bag up all the spoiled foods. A depressing job. Looking on the bright side, at least the freezers and fridges got well defrosted and cleaned out.

MINOR PROBLEMS

A rather minor disaster was the case of the fish head. I had been asked if I would cater for a cold buffet for a customer, which I had gladly agreed to do. Cold poached salmon was to be on the menu. The fish was duly cooked and left to cool, covered on the side. I slipped out to do some shopping, probably cash-and-carry, and on my return Dawn said: "I've skinned the fish and cut off its head and put it in the fridge for you."

"Where's the head?" I said.

"Oh, in the bin of course," was the reply.

Rob opening champagne and spraying the guests

Now when serving salmon I like to leave the head on, so I was slightly dismayed. After thanking Dawn for efficiently putting the fish away, I went to the telephone to ring the local fishmonger.

"Hello, Peter," I said. "I wonder if you can help me?" and I explained the situation.

"Do you have a spare fish head," I asked. "A large fish head," thinking that a herring's head might look a trifle silly!

There was a pause. "Well, I've got a cod's head. Will that do?" It would. I collected it on the way to work the next day, poached it and placed it at the top of the salmon.

The fish went out beautifully decorated with a collar of mayonnaise and parsley. No one would have known the difference.

Another memorable disaster was when I spent all morning making an extremely complex Tiramisu. It went on forever, melting this, soaking that. I think an egg custard was involved. Finally it was completed. With great pride I picked up the glass container to take it to the fridge when it slipped through my fingers, the dish smashing into hundreds of pieces. I was not happy – I probably put a mocha sundae on instead. I certainly didn't make a replacement Tiramisu.

Juliet, on carrying a large glass jar of mayonnaise, had a similar experience. Just as she got to the fridge, the jar slipped. Mayonnaise absolutely everywhere. Bless her, she stood looking at the mess in horror but all she said was: "Oh my word, oh my word." It was a catch phrase in the kitchen for many years.

Mr A, a customer of long standing, rang and booked for lunch. "A special occasion," he said, "my son has just got engaged and we are bringing him and his fiancée to lunch to celebrate."

The day arrived and Mr A asked for champagne. This was duly taken out with the superior flutes and a white linen cloth around the bottle. Now Rob rather prides himself on the discreet manner with which he opens a champagne bottle (after all he has had a lot of practice!). Making much of the situation, cracking a joke, no doubt, and not paying full attention to what he was doing, he gently took the wire off the cork. With a loud pop the cork flew out and the champagne went absolutely everywhere.

"A lively bottle," said Mr A.

Rob was mortified and suitably abject in his apologies. Luckily it was all taken in good part.

One wet afternoon dear Pat got slightly over-enthusiastic while mopping the floor. She was gesticulating with the mop and the handle smashed a fluorescent light. Now when one of these bulbs breaks it shatters into thousands of little fragments. Luckily it happened at the end of trading so there was no food about, otherwise we should have had a real problem. It was bad enough as it was.

We only had one fire at Mary's and that happened while we were at the cash-and-carry. The girls rang through to get the management to tell us while we were there. Over the tannoy the owners of an obscure sounding café were asked for so we took no notice. Then the voice said Mary's café and we rushed to the office where we were told that there had been a fire. Rob quickly rang the girls but it was all over and dealt with. Evidently a fish fryer had caught fire and one of the girls had called the brigade. Meanwhile with great presence of mind Patricia had got the fire blanket and thrown it over the fryer. Then she turned off the electricity switches which were situated underneath the bench on which the fryers stood. Very coolly done; I hope I would have been as composed. She said afterwards that she was more worried about Rob's reaction than the fire. By the time the brigade arrived all was well. They sprayed a bit of foam about making a mess, congratulated Patricia on her handling of the situation, had a cup of tea and went on their way. By the time we returned it was all done and dusted.

There were only two or three accidents in the kitchen and no very serious ones. In the prep kitchen we had a freestanding trolley where trays brought from the dining room were put before they were cleared and the crocks washed up. Some of the clean washing-up was put there before it went to its rightful home.

It was a cardinal rule that if a full tray was brought in from the dining room or garden it should be cleared at once. On busy days the washer-up would be heard to bellow: "Clear your trays." The rejoinder would be: "I will in a minute but I must get an order." I have to say Rob was the worst offender! But I digress.

When Erna, one of my senior girls, was on duty, things went pretty smoothly as she was very efficient. On the offending trolley were a few clean things waiting to be put away, among them the blade from the food processor. Erna came in from the dining room with a full tray and tripped. Trying to save the china she knocked the trolley. The blade flew up in the air and landed on her wrist giving her a very nasty cut, narrowly missing her artery. We ferried her to hospital forthwith.

At the end of trading, everything had to be cleaned down. The least favourite job was cleaning the loos so a rota was put into effect. Scott got himself a container of water from the still and a pair of rubber gloves and went off to do his stint, placing the container on the floor. Jason, his mate, went out to 'help' and of course a bit of horseplay ensued and Scott stepped back into the scalding water.

Andrew came to work for us for a while on some government scheme. In theory he was learning to be a chef but his concentration level was nil. He was a cheery soul, nonetheless. He cycled from Halesworth come rain or shine and always arrived with a smile.

"Now, Andrew," I would say. "This is how we prepare meat for this dish." He would stand at my elbow to watch. I would concentrate on what I was doing, then I would turn to him and find that he had gone, probably to see what the girls were up to. I might give him an easy task to perform, but he always disappeared half way or even a quarter of the way through it and I would find him chatting to someone. Consequently he got quite a lot of the grotty jobs when I became totally exasperated with him. One was to clean out the wheely bin after it had been emptied.

"Now Andrew – are you listening?"

"Yes," as his eyes darted everywhere but at me.

"Lay the bin on its side – get some hot soapy water, — use the mop and clean it out – I'll show you how," which I did. "Do you understand?"

For three weeks all was well and the bin was cleaned in the correct manner. The fourth week Andrew came running in, his front covered in boiling water. It transpired that instead of placing the bin on its side he had balanced his bucket of water on the rim of the bin and attempted to clean it that way. The inevitable happened and the water went all over him.

Andrew being on a government scheme there was, of course, an official knocking on my door to have an inquiry into the matter. He turned out to be our ex-employee Gerry and was very severe with me, probably getting his own back. My worst sin was that I hadn't got an accident book or at that time a list of dangers in the kitchen. I can see the sense of the accident book. With all the litigation there is about these days we could prove that the correct procedure had been followed.

On driving back to the restaurant one Saturday evening I was slightly disturbed to see my two evening girls driving out of the village at a great rate of knots. They gave me a wave and went on their way. It transpired that Dawn had badly cut her finger while preparing tomatoes. Patricia had not been even mildly sympathetic, saying that Dawn had used a carbon steel knife. "Well, you were using the wrong knife anyway, that knife turns the tomatoes black." Dawn and Mel got back in time for trading!

CUSTOMER CATASTROPHES

One serious episode we experienced was when a gentleman suffered a severe heart attack. It was at the end of lunch and his family were on their own in the small dining room. His wife came to ask if we could help, as he wasn't feeling well. Rob sized up the matter and quickly phoned for a doctor. As luck would have it the doctor was attending a patient in the next road so he was with us in minutes, and he had breathing apparatus in his car. The gentleman's life was saved. If — that little word again — the doctor had been elsewhere or there had been any sort of delay we would have had a corpse on our hands: it was that close.

Luckily for us not many of our customers sustained any injuries at Mary's. Shortly after we had done our alterations an elderly lady used one of the outside loos. On walking out she failed to see that there was a retaining wall up about a foot and walked straight off it. She cut her leg badly but broke no bones. It was just as well her daughter was with her, as she persuaded mother to sit down and wait for the paramedics, otherwise the elderly one was for getting up and going home, not wanting to make a fuss. We also put our oar in, saying that if anyone had an accident on our premises we were obliged to call the ambulance in case of complications — as we had done. She wasn't totally convinced but waited for it to arrive, then she insisted on walking to the vehicle, scorning the stretcher that was offered. They don't make them like that anymore!

The next day we had several people call round to see if we were all right as they had seen the ambulance arrive and hoped it wasn't anything too serious.

Then there are the self-induced illnesses; we were about to close one afternoon when two people walked in with a young lady who was in some distress. Could we help? They had found the girl wandering aimlessly along and had offered her some assistance. The girl could hardly talk coherently. What was wrong? When we got close enough we realised why!

"Where have you come from?" I asked

"Along the road."

"How did you get to Walberswick?"

"I came on a bike."

"Where is the bike?"

"I don't know. I must speak to Ray." She became very agitated.

"Where is he?" I asked.

"I've got a phone number here."

I took it and rang the number and got unobtainable. I returned: "Are you sure this is the right number?"

"Yes. I must speak to Ray."

"Was he with you this afternoon?"

"Yes. Down the road".

We thought we might be getting somewhere. "Were you at the pub?"

She pulled herself up and looked disdainfully at us. "We don't drink in pubs," she said. Her agitation increased and she made reference to pills, then she said: "I must go. I can't stay here."

We had a quick discussion. Clearly she was not fit to be left to wander about alone, especially if she had taken some sort of pills on top of alcohol. It was decided that Rob would ring the police. The good samaritans went on their way after helping me to persuade the girl to sit down in the garden. She didn't want anyone near her so we left her at a garden table and I kept an eye on her from a window. Suddenly she seemed to collapse. We rushed out, but she seemed to be asleep and at that moment our Community WPC turned up. We were never more pleased to see anyone, gladly handing over the responsibility to her. The WPC was concerned about the mention of pills, so once more the ambulance was called.

We never heard another word of who the girl was or where the mysterious Ray had gone.

Another time on returning from a short break we drove into our car park to find a police car about to drive off. Rather alarmed I jumped out of our car and stopped it.

"Is there a problem?" I asked. The police seemed taken aback by this. "I'm the owner of the restaurant. Is there something wrong?"

At this they seemed reassured. "No, nothing for you to worry about. Someone has gone missing and his car was seen in your car park."

The girls told us the story. Two days before, about coffee time, a car drove in and a young man got out and walked away. They thought this a bit of a cheek but assumed that he would probably come in for lunch, but the day progressed and there was no sign of the man. They locked up and went home. There was no sign the next day, and later that morning the police called and told them that the man had walked down to the sea and then walked into it. If the coast guard hadn't been looking he would have been swept away never to be seen again. As it was he was rescued. On being questioned he couldn't remember where he had left his car, just in a car park. The police had been hunting for it and here it was. The day after that the young man turned up with his parents to reclaim it. I was forbidden by the staff to go out and ask him if he had had a nice swim!

In thirteen years of trading I don't think this amount of accidents was bad. The two really bad ones involved Rob and me, and were only vaguely connected with the restaurant.

One busy Friday night when I was in the kitchen on my own, I fried my hand instead of the fish! One should always use two hands to place a fish fillet into hot oil in a frying pan – I used one hand, the fish slipped and in trying to save it, in went the palm of my hand. Luckily it was nearly the end of the session and it was my left hand, so I could continue clasping ice cubes on the burn. Rob phoned the local hospital to see where I should go to have it seen to. As it was before midnight I could go to the cottage hospital at Beccles about ten miles away, where I was treated at once by an extremely nice doctor. He put a steroid cream on my hand and gave me some surgical gloves to wear the next day. He was very concerned that he had no strong painkillers.

"Oh," I said blithely. "That's all right. I'll take some of my husband's pethidine."

The doctor looked slightly taken aback. "I think I had better have a word with your husband."

Rob then explained that he had a spastic colon and when it went into a bad spasm he had to take one of the pills. I was instructed to take two when I got home. Now Rob had always said that the effect of the pills was wonderful, like floating on air, so relaxing, and so on. In spite of the pain I was quite looking forward to this. On returning, Rob sat me in a chair, got me a drink, and gave me the pills. There I sat all expectant. Nothing – absolutely nothing – but I did sleep well. I was slightly concerned about the next day: there was a busy lunch booked and I knew that heat on a burn is very painful, but the cream was wonderful. I put some more on in the morning and covered it with a dressing and a glove. There was no pain and no sign of the burn. Magic!

For some time Rob had been suffering from a hernia. The year before he had had one and because it occurred in the spring we had it fixed privately so that he would be fighting fit for the season. The second one popped out in October, so we decided he would wait on the NHS, joining the emergency list for day patients. The call came on a Monday. Could he come in? It was our last week of full-time trading before we began winter opening hours. For some reason our car wasn't available, so I had to drive him up to Norwich in my little blue catering van.

Pennie had been staying for the weekend and came with us in her car before driving back to Lancaster. We duly delivered Rob to the waiting room, saw him fetchingly dressed in an operating gown and went to have a coffee while he had his op. At the appointed hour we were allowed to go and see him. Still under the influence of the drugs he was remarkably cheerful. I went to get my van and reversed it up to the door, where Rob was waiting. 'Felicity's Fare, catering for all occasions' was emblazoned over the side, but this was an 'occasion' I hadn't reckoned on.

The second traumatic accident happened to me. The week passed with Rob recuperating at home from his hernia op and Gem and I going into work. By Thursday Rob seemed to think that he would be well enough to come into work the next day.

"No," I said. "Certainly not, and we can manage without you over the weekend." Ha!

I duly went off to work. At the end of the day while the girls were clearing up, I said that I would take Gem for a walk. Although it was grey and mizzling it was quite mild and very pleasant. "Well, Gem," I said, as one does to one's dog. "I think we'll go a little further than our usual round."

We set off over the common and into the reed beds turning towards Hoist Covert, half a mile from the village. Here the path became very muddy and a large puddle appeared between me and the board walk. Of course I only had shoes on instead of boots, so I tried to circumnavigate the puddle by walking on the edge. My foot slipped and there was an ominous crack.

"Oh no!" I groaned. " I think I've broken my leg." I had never broken a bone, but somehow I knew. Although I had fallen gracefully onto the bank, not into the puddle, the question was: what to do? I had no mobile phone in those days. Daylight was fading fast and the mizzle had become drizzle. I managed to stand up and stagger a few steps but I could go no further, not because of the pain but because I felt so faint and I was afraid I might be doing further damage to my leg. I sat down, Gem beside me looking slightly puzzled. Missus didn't usually behave like this on walks. I became aware of voices coming nearer. Afraid that the owners might go straight on rather than take my path I stood up and called out.

"Excuse me – I wonder if you could help me?" I ask you; how genteel.

A lady and a young man appeared.

"I think I've broken my leg," I whimpered.

The young man took charge. It turned out he was a police officer on holiday with his family – he and his mother had decided to walk back from Dunwich while the rest of the family had gone back by car. He sat me down again on his coat, took off his rucksack and told me to put my leg up – a command I was going to hear a lot. He left his mother with me while he ran back to the restaurant. The story goes that he rushed into the kitchen.

"I've found a lady in the wood with a broken leg."

The staff were vaguely bemused, wondering why the young man was telling *them* about it. Although they were becoming vaguely worried about my non-appearance, they didn't put the two incidents together. They were soon to be told. Patricia phoned for an ambulance. Unfortunately she got the name of the road wrong and while I lay in the wood I could hear the ambulance driving around, siren sounding, but not coming near me.

Eventually I was located. The young man returned and must have looked after Gem. The men drove the ambulance as near to me as they could, placed me on a stretcher and tried to get me into the van. Unfortunately it was parked on "the huh" so the stretcher wouldn't clip in. Finally after much banging I was put in place. Then of course there was the form to fill in and I thought I was on my way to hospital. Not so. When we reached the A12 we stopped in a layby. The men who had picked me up had finished their shift and they were waiting for their relief to take over. And here we sat until the relief turned up – they had been told that the accident had happened at the bird reserve, so had gone a twisty six miles to

Minsmere. Finally the change-over took place and *another* form had to be filled in. While we were completing this, there was a tap on the door and a head appeared.

"Have you got Mrs Jelliff in here?" said a voice. It was Tracey, one of my girls.

She had come to ask if I would like her to come to the hospital after she had taken Gem home and told Rob what had transpired. Would I! "What hospital are you going to?"

In one voice the ambulance man and I said: "James Paget" (Great Yarmouth) and "Ipswich."

"Well, which?" Tracey asked. The choice was mine as we were on the half-way mark, so James Paget it was. Tracey went on her way and finally so did I – but no flashing blue light for me.

I arrived at the hospital and was taken to casualty where after an initial assessment I was left. Later I was told that a man was suffering a heart attack so all was forgiven. But it would have been nice to be told at the time. Suddenly there were Tracey and Rob. The latter had got off his sick bed to come and see me. They stood around until a doctor appeared who thought that the leg was broken and I would have to go and have an x-ray. I was concerned that Tracey was having to do a lot of hanging about, but the doctor told us not to worry, he would organise transport to take Rob and me home. Ha! So Tracey left us. I was duly taken to x-ray – yes, the leg *was* broken but no, they couldn't plaster it because the plasterer had gone home. Back to casualty where two delightful nurses put a back plaster and splints on my leg.

"How are you getting home? Is your husband driving you?"

We explained that Rob had just had a hernia op and wouldn't be able to drive for three weeks.

"Not to worry," I said. "The doctor said that he would organise a car for us."

They looked concerned. "He won't have done that." He hadn't. "You will have to wait two hours for any transport we might get you.

Can't you ring a friend?"

Yes but who? Several of our friends would be into the second glass of wine at that time and we had no telephone numbers with us. Tracey had left her number with us in case of problems. Bless her – we now *had* a problem. Rob phoned Tracey. Yes, of course she would come back and get us but could she just have a cup of coffee as she had only just got home, having been told she wasn't needed.

The next day I had to go back to hospital to be plastered and kind neighbours took us in their camper van, so I was able to travel on one of the beds. More x-rays and finally I was encased in plaster. It was a worry, as the doctor wanted to make sure I didn't need a pin as it was a nasty long break. I didn't want to have to stay in hospital and luckily no pin was required.

Of course it was a lovely day, our staff had to cope without us and, of course, the world fell in on them. If they had to wait after a hurried explanation, our customers were very understanding. Only two people walked out. So poor old Rob had to go into work that weekend after all. My little dog was very funny. Because of the leg, for the first two nights I slept downstairs, Gem beside me on her beanbag. Saturday morning dawned and Rob's lift arrived. "Come on, Gem," he said. Gem turned her back and refused to leave me. I was very touched, as she loved to go to work. The next morning the same procedure happened but I could tell that this time she was tempted, so I said: "Off you go, Gem." Away she went, albeit reluctantly.

Staffing was a bit of a problem at this time. Rob had to be ferried to and fro and there was the small difficulty of getting cover for me. Luckily November was usually a quiet month so Patricia was able to cope with the lunches on Fridays and Saturdays. Sundays were covered by Bea, a lady who had joined the team as a cake cook. She had retired from her own business so that she could have Sundays off so it was very noble of her to come in. Dinners we knocked on the head for six weeks. Financially not a good time, especially as being self-employed there was no sick pay for me.

The weeks passed and after two weeks I went into work, polishing glasses and cutlery, and other chores that could be done sitting down. At last, two weeks before Christmas, it was time for the plaster to come off. The cast was sawn away and another x-ray taken, then a wait to see the doctor. He wasn't pleased with the way the break was mending.

"I would like to see you in a month's time," he said.

"Oh," said I. "I can't come then. I shall be in Africa." "No," said the doctor. "That wouldn't be wise."

"And what's more," I countered. "I have to cook Christmas lunch for forty people."

He looked very severe. "You either cook the meal and don't go to Africa or you get someone else to cook the meal and go to Africa."

I did both. I was told to continue using the crutches and a great nuisance they were, too. Wherever I put them they would fall down or trip someone up, usually Rob.

Christmas lunch went well. That year friends were roped in with their son and daughter, along with Pennie and her fiancé Paul. After the meal was completed I went upstairs to the flat to put the leg up as I had been instructed. Before they went home most of our customers trooped upstairs to say thank you. I sat there like some minor royal receiving homage!

There were no repercussions from this, so we felt encouraged to risk the flight to Namibia. We talked to our doctor, to the physiotherapist, and to another doctor at the hospital. No one would commit himself, just told me to keep the leg up. Now I realise that it was deep vein thrombosis they were worried about, but no one said so at the time. We were *emphatic* that we were going as it was a trip long in the planning – we were to meet Colin, Di, Judy, Barbara and a friend at Jo'burg on the plane to Windhoek where we were to pick up a minibus to tour some of the country for a week.

After which Rob and I were to stay in Jo'burg for a night, before flying to Zimbabwe, hiring a car and driving to Bulawayo and around, before flying home.

Having taken the decision, we rang Emirates, one of our planned airlines, about assisted passage and for a suitable seat for elevating my leg. Emirates couldn't have been more helpful. South African Airways who were our carriers for the later stage, were less so. They even said that it was unlikely that we would catch the connecting flight to Namibia and there wasn't another one until the next day and that was full. Another problem!

We rang the railways in London and locally about an assisted passage; they made lots of rash promises. The time came, our staff were assigned their duties, dog was taken to friends for the duration. We were packed, the house locked up, the taxi arrived and we were off. We boarded the train at Halesworth, setting off for Ipswich where we were met by a charming young girl and a wheelchair and taken the hundred yards up the platform..

At this point I will say that it is perfectly true that once one is put in a wheelchair one becomes invisible or mentally deficient – the 'does she take sugar' syndrome comes into play and one gets pushed into corners and left.

We arrived at Liverpool Street Station on time. Another wheelchair was there to meet us and take us to the taxi rank as at that time I couldn't possibly manage the Underground. The trip to Paddington took forever, but we had allowed plenty of time – just as well. At Paddington I was disposed of in a waiting room with several people all waiting for the one available wheelchair. We waited and waited. Nothing happened and after a while we decided that we would make our own way to our platform, which we did, poor Rob festooned with cases but luckily we managed to hijack the wheelchair on the way!

On arriving at Heathrow there was no sign of any assisted passage, so we struggled up the interminable passage. On arriving in the vicinity of the Emirates check-in point, a wheelchair and a young man arrived from nowhere and we were whisked through all the formalities and into duty free. Here we were left to our own devices until our flight was called, whereupon we were taken to the departure point. When it was time to be wheeled into the plane our young man joined us and gleefully told us that we had been upgraded for the first leg of our flight. Joy!

The wheelchair was there to meet us at Dubai but there was no idle chat here as our Arab helper had no English. He kept leaving me in odd corners until at a great rate of knots he took us to the first-class lounge where we learnt that our flight was to be delayed by an hour. Our hearts sank. We would certainly miss our flight to Namibia. What to do? Wait and see — it was all we could do. We were relegated to cattle class for this part of the journey and I sat with my leg on poor Rob's lap.

As we approached Jo'burg we told our stewardess about our predicament. Would we be allowed out of the plane first, rather than last as was the usual case with assisted passengers. She would see what she could do. A little later she came back.

"The good news is," she said, "that you can get out after the first class passengers if you can manage the stairs." I certainly could. She went on: "The better news is that as we have had a tail wind we've made up the hour. In fact we are going to be early."

Our spirits rose. However: man proposes, God disposes. Indeed, we did get off the plane first and we were met with a wheelchair, but whose cases were the last on to the carousel? And as we were changing airlines the luggage couldn't be booked through. Finally the cases arrived and we had still over half an hour in hand.

"Where do we go now?" Our young wheelchair pusher asked. She was asking *us*?

"Transit passengers must go through security and check in," boomed the tannoy.

Oh no, we thought, but our young lass didn't seem to hear and we went a back way to South African Airways check-in desk. Still half an hour in hand. Rob dashed to the desk. I was left! He seemed to be gesticulating a lot. 'Bad news,' I thought and indeed it was. Rob came back to me. "Was there a problem?" I asked.

"They told me the flight was closed. I told them we hadn't bloody-well flown half way around the world, with you on crutches, to be told that the flight was closed when there was still half an hour to go, so would they open it up and get someone to push you to the plane. So they promised they would!"

As though on cue a young man appeared and we set off at a cracking pace up lifts, down again out on the tarmac, dodging around planes — stationary ones, I hasten to add. Finally we were put on a weird contraption and driven to the side of a plane. Our platform was pumped up. When we were on a level with the side of the plane our young man knocked on a panel which slid open and I was wheeled in – we had made it!

But where was our party? There was no sign of them.

"Do you think they've put us on the wrong plane?" I asked. Rob walked to the front to where a stewardess and possibly the pilot stood.

"Excuse me," he said. "You may think this is a stupid question, but is this plane going to Windhoek?"

"I certainly hope so," came the reply, at which point Judy walked up the stairs. Barbara flew a lot on business so they had all been waiting in the first class lounge — where the flight *hadn't* been called. It was only because Judy had become slightly anxious and walked out into the main hall she had heard them all being paged for the flight.

And we all made it in the end.

It was a great holiday — and I didn't miss much of the activities. I didn't climb Dune Seven, one of the highest in Namibia, which of course I would have done if I had had two whole legs!

Neither was I able to climb up a cliff to see some ancient cave paintings. Saddest of all, I didn't see the desert elephants. The young man who organised that trip was very anxious that I shouldn't go on the safari as the week before a lady had re-broken a wrist on the Land Rover when it had bumped over the rocky terrain. Reluctantly I stayed behind. The others had decided not to tell me that they had seen the elephants, but of course it came out they had. Anyway, it is an excuse to go back. At this camp we slept in *rondavels* the traditional housing of southern Africa. The first night there were lots of munching and strange noises outside. Cautiously we looked out to see what strange animals might be traversing our patch but they were only donkeys.

I *did* manage to climb up to see Rhodes's grave, and I *did* manage the climb to the top of the ruins at Great Zimbabwe. It was marvellous. And on our return I threw the crutches into a corner never to be used again. D.V

CHOCOLATE NUT SUNDAE

Chocolate sauce
Sundae dish
Vanilla ice cream
Chopped nuts
Glacé cherry
Sugar curls　　Cream

METHOD

Swirl chocolate sauce around sundae dish. Place three scoops of ice cream in dish. Cover with a little sauce; scatter some nuts over the whole. Add a whirl of freshly whipped cream. Drizzle with a little chocolate sauce over cream. Sprinkle more nuts. Place a glacé cherry in the centre. Strategically place two sugar curls in the cream..

CHOCOLATE SAUCE

12 oz dark chocolate.
8 z granulated sugar.
½ pint water.

METHOD

Break up chocolate. Place it with the sugar and water into a large saucepan. Put on a low heat to dissolve chocolate and sugar. Then turn up the heat and boil furiously for about ten minutes, less if you are using expensive chocolate. The mixture will boil up and then fall back. This is the time to watch it, making sure you don't make fudge.

AND AFTER

Catering is a difficult business for a couple to work together in and a lot of marriages go by the wayside. Quite often one or other will have an affair with a member of staff or run off with another person. This always amazes Rob and me. Where do they find the time or the energy? The highlight of our week was going to the cash-and-carry together.

It has to be said that running a restaurant becomes a way of life and as it doesn't switch off when you turn the lock, it infringes one's personal life.

On the last night of our famous holiday in the Seychelles we treated ourselves to dinner at a lovely restaurant by the ocean — palm trees, moonlight, the lot. We had nearly finished our meal when we became aware of the party at the next table. The words Southwold and Beccles came drifting across the Indian Ocean. As we left, we introduced ourselves. One of the men had just moved his dental practice from Southwold to the Seychelles island of Praslin. His guests were visiting him and yes, they knew Mary's very well.

In a hotel in Cape Town I got out of the lift and was making my way towards the restaurant when I realised that Rob was no longer with me. Turning, I saw that he was talking to two strangers, but no, they were Mary's regular customers.Our trip then took us on to Rorke's Drift where we had a busy day touring the Zulu War battlefield, after which we went to our lodge, bathed and returned to the dining room where we ensconced ourselves at the communal trestle table. A rather nice man on my left asked me where I came from and what I did for a living.

"Oh," I said. " My husband and I run a restaurant." I never mentioned I was a cook in case there was a crisis in the kitchen.

"Whereabouts was it?"

"In a little Suffolk village called Walberswick and the name of the restaurant was Mary's."

At which point a voice on my right said in a rather accusing voice: "I know it. Last summer we came for a visit and you wouldn't give us dinner because you said you were full." I found myself saying apologetically that if I had said we were full, I am sure we would have been.

I had a short stay in Gorleston Hospital, all of five hours for a very minor 'op'. I hadn't recovered long from the anaesthetic when the sister's voice came across the ward.

"I know you. You're the lady from Mary's." Groggily I agreed that I was.

A year before we retired, Pennie was married in Lancaster. With our strong team in place we were able to have several days up north to be with her. She and Paul had their wedding reception at Leighton Hall, a dream location for the event. The gardens were beautiful and we were able to enjoy them in the early summer sunshine. As well as letting out the hall for receptions, the owner, Mrs Reynolds, kept several species of raptors and kept them for flying displays. Members of the public could book and spend a day learning about falconry. Rob has always had a great respect for falcons and owls, and in passing he expressed an interest in visiting the hall. The 'children' homed in on this and for a birthday present they paid for Rob to have a day's instruction.

On the morning of his arrival he learned how to tie a falconer's knot, to place a jessie on a bird, and even how to handle one or two of the falcons.

Came the afternoon and a public display: Rob was an assistant. A Harris's hawk that he had handled that morning, was used, and afterwards he was tidying up when he heard someone say: "It *is* you, Rob. I couldn't believe my eyes. The last time I saw you you were passing me a glass of wine. Whatever are you doing here?"
Rob turned to see a customer, one who had moved from Suffolk to Kirkby Lonsdale a few years previously. On a whim he had decided to spend the afternoon at Leighton Hall. He was very surprised to see Rob handling the hawk with such dexterity. Certainly a change from a wine bottle!

When we were on winter opening hours we had the telephone put through to our home. That way people could book for the restaurant rather than leave a message on the answerphone. When it did ring one could be quite sure that it would be at the most inopportune times. The most traumatic was the evening my mother was dying and we were waiting desperately for the doctor to call.

"Can I book a table for four on Sunday?" came the voice. I hope we were polite.

Poor soul, she couldn't have known what we were going through.

Being mostly in the kitchen I didn't meet people in the way Rob did, so I didn't always recognise customers when we were out. As my eyesight began to fade I was apt to walk about with a silly smile on my face so that I wouldn't offend.

On one famous occasion I was stopped by a man in the street. Thinking that he must be a customer I entered a long and involved conservation about people I had never heard of, but I thought that I should have done, so I gave vague, noncommittal replies. It slowly dawned on the man I was not the person he thought I was and he had certainly never been to Mary's. I didn't know who felt the more foolish.

More than once we would be accosted with: "You don't know who we are, but we came to Mary's quite often."

Rob, of course, would respond with a smile and say of course he remembered them, while I stood twitching in the background. He was an extremely good front man. He enjoyed meeting the customers and chatting to them, never appearing to be bored even when they were explaining to him how they had installed their shower in every minute detail.

I would mutter as I passed him: "Stop chatting. Table five needs seeing to."

It wasn't that I didn't like people, I was always concentrating on the kitchen and the problems that arose there. As when one of the girls came in to me and said: "There is a gluten-free vegan with an allergy to nuts on table nine. What can they have?"

"Right," I said "I will go and see them." Into the dining room I marched to be met by my son who had come down unexpectedly. He told me he had heard my remark ringing from the kitchen and it had definitely sounded like a threat.

FAREWELL, MARYS!

Our last few weeks at the restaurant were great fun. Dirk, the young man who was buying Mary's came to work for us, taking the opportunity to learn the ropes. He was an excellent chef so that freed me up from the kitchen and I joined Rob in the restaurant. It turned into a double act, daily becoming more and more like Fawlty Towers.

Suddenly it was our last weekend. Obviously we had told our regulars that we had sold. Consequently on that weekend we were very busy. In fact tables were by invitation only and with so many old friends it was like one continual party. On the Saturday evening we had invited all our close family to dinner. This we had in the flat, making our poor boys and girls stagger upstairs with our meals. While we were sitting over coffee the door burst open and there were all our customers who had been dining below come to say farewell. A poem was read and a song was sung. Tears all around.

And so after buying Mary's on the thirteenth of March, running it for thirteen years, then selling on to Dirk on the thirteenth of June, we have retired. What are we doing now? Well, a bit of this and a bit of that. Rob is fast becoming a master of wine as he is in a sea of blackberry, raspberry, apple and elderberry wine. He is on the Village Common Committee and drives the community bus. I still do a little outside catering, although I'm not sure if providing food for a black tie dinner for 140 in a circus tent or making a thousand mince-pies at Christmas actually counts as a little. The garden keeps us busy, especially as we have recently acquired an adjacent piece of land which we are turning into a vegetable patch. Now we can enjoy the products of our labours. We have adopted a very large, very boisterous, very hairy dog who has proved to be a bit of a culture shock after quiet little Gem. When we took him in he was already christened Ged, consequently was called Gem more than once. He takes us for long walks which we trust will keep us fit. Ged would not have fitted into Mary's at all! He would probably have knocked customers over, waved his hairy tail in the soup and produced chewed, slobbery balls at inopportune moments.

One good thing about retirement is that when I have to fill in official forms or landing cards that ask for occupation I no longer have the embarrassment of having to ask how to spell *restaurateur*. When we were in an African state I consoled myself that they probably couldn't spell it either. Now I can simply put 'retired' and even *I* can spell that.

The restaurant already seems to have been another life. Occasionally we meet youngsters and say: "You look familiar. Have we met before?" They reply: "Well, yes. You employed me for two years." It has happened. When we meet ex-customers, and depending on how he feels, Rob will deny owning Mary's, saying that was his brother and yes they do look alike.

I look back over the years that we ran the business and I have to conclude that we have made lots of friends, we've achieved financial stability, and retired with many happy memories. Yes, we were a success. However, I haven't been able to free myself from my two *bêtes noires*. My daughter and my mother-in-law are vegetarians and Rob insists on custard with his blackberry and apple crumble.

Do we miss it? Oh yes! I should say so. When it is a sunny Sunday and we are lying in our loungers with a Pimms to hand, we visualise the gridlock that can be Walberswick's main street and we miss it!! Then we will recall those high days and holidays when there were dockets up to the ceilings, queues at the back door, queues at the front door, when every surface was covered with dirty crocks and we would look at each other and say: "Isn't this the most tremendous fun?"

And it was – wasn't it?